conne

BIBLE STUDY GUIDE
LARGE PRINT EDITION

On Your Mark
The Gospel in Motion

A STUDY OF THE
Gospel of Mark

Ed Jordan
Jesse Rincones
Wesley Shotwell
Julie Wood

DISCOVER
BIBLE
STUDY
GUIDE
BELIEVE
LIVE

BaptistWayPress®
Dallas, Texas

BAPTISTWAY PRESS® Leadership Team
Executive Director, Baptist General Convention of Texas: David Hardage
Director, Great Commission Team: Delvin Atchison
Publisher, BaptistWay Press®: Scott Stevens

Cover: Micah Kandros Design
Interior Design and Production: Desktop Miracles, Inc.
Printing: Data Reproductions Corporation

First edition: December 2016
ISBN–13: 978–1–938355–65–3

How to Make the Best Use of This Issue

Whether you're the teacher or a student—

1. Start early in the week before your class meets.

2. Overview the study. Review the table of contents and read the study introduction. Try to see how each lesson relates to the overall study.

3. Use your Bible to read and consider prayerfully the Scripture passages for the lesson. (You'll see that each writer has chosen a favorite translation for the lessons in this issue. You're free to use the Bible translation you prefer and compare it with the translation chosen for that unit, of course.)

4. After reading all the Scripture passages in your Bible, then read the writer's comments. The comments are intended to be an aid to your study of the Bible.

5. Read the small articles—"sidebars"—in each lesson. They are intended to provide additional, enrichment information and inspiration and to encourage thought and application.

6. Try to answer for yourself the questions included in each lesson. They're intended to encourage further

thought and application, and they can also be used in the class session itself.

If you're the teacher—
Do all of the things just mentioned, of course. As you begin the study with your class, be sure to find a way to help your class know the date on which each lesson will be studied. Here are some suggestions to guide your lesson preparation:

A. In the first session of the study, briefly overview the study by identifying for your class the date on which each lesson will be studied. Lead your class to write the date in the table of contents on page 9 and on the first page of each lesson.

   - Make and post a chart that indicates the date on which each lesson will be studied.
   - If all of your class has e-mail, send them an e-mail with the dates the lessons will be studied.
   - Provide a bookmark with the lesson dates. You may want to include information about your church and then use the bookmark as an outreach tool, too. A model for a bookmark can be downloaded from www.baptistwaypress.org under the "Teacher Helps" menu.
   - Develop a sticker with the lesson dates, and place it on the table of contents or on the back cover.

B. Get a copy of the *Teaching Guide*, a companion piece to this *Study Guide*. The *Teaching Guide* contains additional Bible comments plus two teaching plans. The teaching plans in the *Teaching Guide* are intended to provide practical, easy-to-use teaching suggestions that will work in your class.

C. After you've studied the Bible passage, the lesson comments, and other material, use the teaching suggestions in the *Teaching Guide* to help you develop your plan for leading your class in studying each lesson.

D. Teaching resource items for use as handouts are available free at www.baptistwaypress.org under the "Teacher Helps" tab.

E. Additional Bible study comments on the lessons are available online. Call 1–866–249–1799 or e-mail baptistway@texasbaptists.org to order the *Premium Commentary*. It is available only in electronic format (PDF) from our website, www.baptistwaypress.org. The price of these comments for the entire study is $5 per person. A church or class that participates in our advance order program for free shipping can receive the *Premium Commentary* free. Call 1–866–249–1799 or see www.baptistwaypress.org to purchase or for information on participating in our free shipping program for the next study.

F. Additional teaching plans are also available in electronic format (PDF) by calling 1–866–249–1799. The price of these additional teaching plans for the entire study is $5 per person. A church or class that participates in our advance order program for free shipping can receive the *Premium Teaching Plans* free. Call 1–866–249–1799 or see www.baptistwaypress.org for information on participating in our free shipping program for the next study.

G. Enjoy leading your class in discovering the meaning of the Scripture passages and in applying these passages to their lives.

Do you use a Kindle?

This Connect 360 *Bible Study Guide*, along with several other studies, is available in a Kindle edition. The easiest way to find these materials is to search for "BaptistWay" on your Kindle, or go to www.amazon.com/kindle and do a search for "BaptistWay." The Kindle edition can be studied not only on a Kindle but also on your smartphone or tablet using the Kindle app available free from amazon.com/kindle.

Writers for This *Study Guide*

Jesse Rincones wrote **lessons one through four**. Jesse is the Executive Director of the Hispanic Baptist Convention of Texas. He earned a bachelor's degree in Mathematics and a Doctor of Jurisprudence from Texas Tech University. Jesse serves on the boards of the Baptist University of the Americas, the Baptist Joint Committee's Religious Liberty Council and the National Hispanic Christian Leadership Conference.

Julie (Brown) Wood wrote **lessons five through seven**. Julie is a graduate of Hardin-Simmons University and Southwestern Baptist Theological Seminary. Having recently moved from East Texas (Jacksonville) to West Texas, she loves ministering with her husband, Dr. Darin Wood, senior pastor of First Baptist Church, in Midland, Texas; and being mother to their son, Joshua. A former children's minister and worship leader, she now serves as a freelance writer and accompanist.

Ed Jordan wrote **lessons eight through ten**. Dr. Jordan is a graduate of Golden Gate Baptist Theological Seminary. He served with the International Mission Board in Leadership Development, Theological Education, and Curriculum Development in Hungary after the fall of the Iron Curtain.

He has written and edited a 52-lesson curriculum for new church plants and two hermeneutic books. He writes a weekly award-winning column for the Idaho State Journal, a quarterly column for the Danville Register & Bee's Southern Virginia Living Magazine, a weekly blog for the Baptist General Association of Virginia (BGAV.org), and a quarterly column for the BGAV Express. He and his wife live in Virginia where he serves as the pastor of Gwynn's Island Baptist Church.

Wesley Shotwell wrote **lessons eleven through thirteen and the Christmas lesson**. Wesley is the pastor of Ash Creek Baptist Church, Azle, Texas. Dr. Shotwell formerly was pastor of churches in Tennessee. He is a graduate of Baylor University (B.A.), Southwestern Baptist Theological Seminary (M.Div.), and Vanderbilt Divinity School (D.Min.).

On Your Mark:
The Gospel in Motion
A Study of the Gospel of Mark

Introducing

On Your Mark:
The Gospel in Motion
A STUDY OF THE GOSPEL OF MARK

Approaching This Study of the Gospel of Mark

Lights, camera, action! Do you enjoy action-packed movies? Stories that reveal incredible strength and uncompromising character? It's one thing when these movies are about fictional characters in imaginary places, but quite another when the story is about a real person overcoming incredible odds or displaying amazing courage and sacrifice in the real world.

If you like such films, you are in for a treat. The Gospel of Mark is an action-packed story of the ministry of Jesus. The Gospel covers the three-and-one-half years of Jesus' public ministry and reveals him as both a miracle worker and a supernatural servant. He is constantly on the move preaching, teaching, healing, and preparing his disciples to carry the gospel forward following his death and resurrection.

Mark focuses on Jesus' actions rather than his words. He records eighteen of Jesus' miracles while only mentioning four of his parables. These miracles revealed Jesus' divine identity and his supernatural power.

Perhaps you've heard the saying that some people watch things happen and some people make things happen. Jesus made things happen. He put the gospel in motion. Jesus moved to where the people were who needed him. He healed people so they could move. He moved people physically, mentally, emotionally, and spiritually; and he still does.

And we will have to move to follow him.

This study of the Gospel of Mark will challenge us to get involved in keeping the gospel in motion as we view the ministry of Jesus though a biblical lens. Get ready for an incredible ride!

More on Mark

No matter how good our motivation is, we likely do not approach the Gospel of Mark with the same level of interest, and certainly not the same sense of urgency, that those who first read it did. For one thing, we likely think we already know much of the story of Jesus. So now we're just going over it one more time. It will be good to do that, we're sure, but we're really pretty familiar with it.

And, do we have a sense of urgency about our Christian faith? Probably not. Mark's first readers, though, lived in threatening and difficult days. They may have been facing persecution in Rome during the middle and latter part of the decade of the 60s. In such a situation, they needed to know what kind of person and message could demand their devotion even to the point of giving their lives. We—particularly North American Christians—though, tend to live more or less comfortable lives. Many seem to think they should get some sort of prize for discipleship just because they attend church fairly regularly.

If these are our thoughts, we're mistaken. We've likely not absorbed fully the challenging nature of who Jesus is. Likely, too, we've not caught up to Jesus' demands of those who would be his disciples and we've ignored Jesus' call to us to participate in his mission in our world.

The Gospel of Mark presents Jesus as being radically different from what the people of his day expected. Once we get to know Jesus as the Gospel of Mark presents him, we may well think that that's still the case.

The first verse of Mark describes Jesus as "the Messiah, the Son of God" (Mark 1:1). The rest of the Gospel of Mark verifies and clarifies in many ways what that means—not just theologically but personally. Be prepared to affirm or re-affirm what that means for you as you study these lessons.

Since the beginning of our BaptistWay Bible study series, we have focused on the Book of Mark three previous times (the last time was in 2012.)[1]

We think studying Scriptures directly about Jesus on a regular basis is important, so we provide a study of a Gospel each year. Each study begins with a new emphasis and fresh outlines and lessons are created.

A Little Background on the Gospel of Mark

The Gospel of Mark likely is the first written Gospel, probably appearing some thirty-five or so years after Jesus' death and resurrection. The early Christian preachers had preached the gospel, and now Mark wrote down the message that had been proclaimed about Jesus through the decades. In fact, the Gospel of Mark may well reflect Peter's preaching, as many Bible commentators suggest.

Mark's first readers might have been facing persecution in Rome during the middle of the 60s. In such a situation, a decision had to be made about Jesus. Christians needed to know what kind of person and message could demand their devotion even to the point of calling for their lives. Prospective Christians needed this information, too, as they pondered whether committing their lives to Jesus was worth it. Moreover, as the eyewitnesses to Jesus' earthly life began to pass away, these early Christians also needed information they could share with others and so lead them to commitment to Jesus.

The Gospel of Mark in Our Day

How should the Gospel of Mark impact Jesus' followers today? A study of Mark gives us the opportunity to evaluate how involved we are in keeping the gospel in motion. Are we willing to take personal risks to bring the gospel to our relationships with acts of sacrifice and service? As Jesus said in correcting the disciples' notion of greatness,

> Jesus called them together and said, "You know that those who are regarded as rulers of the Gentiles lord it over them, and their high officials exercise authority over them. Not so with you. Instead, whoever wants to become great among you must be your servant, and whoever wants to be first must be slave of all. For even the Son of Man did not come to be served, but to serve, and to give his life as a ransom for many. (Mark 10:42–45)

In addition, Jesus laid out the expectations of discipleship:

> Then he called the crowd to him along with his disciples and said: "Whoever wants to be my disciple must deny themselves and take up their cross and follow me. For whoever wants to save their life will lose it, but whoever loses their life for me and for the gospel will save it. What good is it for someone to gain the whole world, yet forfeit their soul? Or what can anyone give in exchange for their soul? If

anyone is ashamed of me and my words in this adulterous and sinful generation, the Son of Man will be ashamed of them when he comes in his Father's glory with the holy angels. (Mark 8:34–38)

Our prayer is that this study of the Gospel of Mark will motivate us all to be actively involved in propelling the gospel forward in the settings and relationships where God has placed us.

**ON YOUR MARK: THE GOSPEL IN MOTION
A STUDY OF THE GOSPEL OF MARK**

Additional Resources for Studying the *Gospel of Mark*[2]

William Barclay. *The Gospel of Mark*. Revised edition. Philadelphia: The Westminster Press, 1975.

Bruce Barton, Philip Comfort, Grant Osborne, Linda K. Taylor, and Dave Veerman. *Life Application New Testament Commentary*. Carol Stream, Illinois: Tyndale House Publishers, Inc., 2001.

James A. Brooks. *Mark*. The New American Commentary. Volume 23. Nashville, Tennessee: Broadman Press, 1991.

Sharyn Dowd. *Reading Mark: A Literary and Theological Commentary on the Second Gospel*. Reading the New Testament Series. Macon, Georgia: Smyth and Helwys Publishing, 2000.

David E. Garland. *Mark*. The NIV Application Commentary. Grand Rapids, Michigan: Zondervan Publishing House, 1996.

Craig S. Keener. *IVP Bible Background Commentary: New Testament*. Downers Grove, Illinois: InterVarsity Press, 1993.

William L. Lane. *The Gospel According to Mark*. The New International Commentary on the New Testament. Grand Rapids, Michigan: William B. Eerdmans Publishing Company, 1974.

Tremper Longmann III and David E. Garland – General Editors. *Expositor's Bible Commentary* – Revised Edition 9, Matthew-Mark. Grand Rapids, Michigan: Zondervan, electronic edition.

Lloyd J. Ogilvie. *Life Without Limits*: Waco, Texas: Word Books, Publisher, 1975.

Pheme Perkins. "Mark." *The New Interpreter's Bible*, Volume VIII. Nashville, Tennessee: Abingdon Press, 1995.

A. T. Robertson. *Word Pictures in the New Testament*. Volume I. Nashville, Tennessee: Broadman Press, 1930.

Notes

1. See www.baptistwaypress.org.
2. Listing a book does not imply full agreement by the writers or BAPTISTWAY PRESS® with all of its comments.

lesson  1

Exercising Spiritual Authority

MAIN IDEA

Jesus displayed his spiritual authority by teaching those who listened, healing the afflicted, and defeating demons.

QUESTION TO EXPLORE

How can we recognize and respond to Jesus' spiritual authority in our lives?

STUDY AIM

To recognize and respond to Jesus' spiritual authority in my life

QUICK READ

Jesus exercised supernatural authority that generated practical results in the lives of those who listened to him, the people he healed, and those he set free from evil spirits. We, too, can experience the power of Jesus' authority in our lives.

Introduction

"This one looks good, Dad; it has car chases and explosions!" My daughter Kimberly was researching potential movies as we contemplated an afternoon of popcorn and Icees® at our local theater. I love movies filled with adventure, as Kimberly well knows. For me, nothing compares to the nonstop thrill ride of an action-packed film.

The Book of Mark could be considered the action-adventure Gospel. Focusing more on the miracles of Jesus than his parables, this disciple was clearly interested in the actions of Jesus. Given the opportunity to title his Gospel, Mark might have chosen a spin-off of the "Acts of the Apostles" and gone with "The Acts of the Divine."

The significant difference between the action in a blockbuster film and the action described in the Gospel of Mark is simple and personal. I will probably never hang from a spinning helicopter in an attempt to bring down a rogue secret agent. I doubt I will ever maneuver a high-performance sports car on a wild chase through the hairpin turns of the Swiss Alps. However, I have experienced the powerful authority of Jesus. You can too. In fact, for the next several lessons, we will join Mark and experience the adventures of Jesus.

Like an action flick that opens with fast-paced scenes, pounding music, and special effects, the first chapter of Mark begins with eye-opening drama.[1]

Mark 1:21–39

21 They went to Capernaum, and when the Sabbath came, Jesus went into the synagogue and began to teach. **22** The people were amazed at his teaching, because he taught them as one who had authority, not as the teachers of the law. **23** Just then a man in their synagogue who was possessed by an evil spirit cried out, **24** "What do you want with us, Jesus of Nazareth? Have you come to destroy us? I know who you are—the Holy One of God!"

25 "Be quiet!" said Jesus sternly. "Come out of him!" **26** The evil spirit shook the man violently and came out of him with a shriek.

27 The people were all so amazed that they asked each other, "What is this? A new teaching—and with authority! He even gives orders to evil spirits and they obey him." **28** News about him spread quickly over the whole region of Galilee.

29 As soon as they left the synagogue, they went with James and John to the home of Simon and Andrew. **30** Simon's mother-in-law was in bed with a fever, and they told Jesus about her. **31** So he went to her, took her hand and helped her up. The fever left her and she began to wait on them.

32 That evening after sunset the people brought to Jesus all the sick and demon-possessed. **33** The whole town gathered at the door, **34** and Jesus healed many who had various diseases. He also drove out many demons, but he would not let the demons speak because they knew who he was.

35 Very early in the morning, while it was still dark, Jesus got up, left the house and went off to a solitary place, where he prayed. **36** Simon and his companions went to look for

21

him,[37] and when they found him, they exclaimed: "Everyone is looking for you!"

[38] Jesus replied, "Let us go somewhere else—to the nearby villages—so I can preach there also. That is why I have come." [39] So he traveled throughout Galilee, preaching in their synagogues and driving out demons.

Authority Speaks (1:21–22)

A typical Sunday morning in my home goes like this: Somebody oversleeps. A shoe is missing. Pants need ironing. Someone is eating breakfast in the church parking lot. When my crew finally makes it through the church doors, we find comfort in familiar heartfelt prayers, beautiful music, encouraging Scripture readings, and, of course, a powerful sermon.

The Jews who attended the synagogue on the Sabbath described in Mark 1 probably expected a familiar worship experience, including a religious leader delivering a customary teaching. However, on that Sabbath day, things were different. The teacher was a young and revolutionary rabbi named Jesus. As worshippers listened intently, they quickly realized the teaching on that Sabbath day was dramatically different from any they had ever heard. The teacher was different. What he said was different. And how he said it was drastically different.

Mark tells us, "The people were amazed at his teaching because he taught them as one who had authority" (1:22).

The listeners in the synagogue experienced the power of spiritual authority in the truth and teachings of Jesus Christ. They were astonished at Jesus' authority.

You and I should not be surprised by this power. Today, we know what those in Capernaum that Sabbath day did not realize. We know the truth Jesus declared before leaving earth: "All authority in heaven and on earth has been given to me" (Matthew 28:18). Jesus' words on that Sabbath day reflected the authority he received from God the Father.

Do you recognize the groundbreaking authority of Jesus' teachings? Have you comprehended that his words differ from the spiritual writings of others? Like the people whom Mark described, do the biblical truths of Jesus amaze you?

A financial analyst's assessment of a company can cause the value of its stock to rise or tank. A judge's ruling can curtail a man's freedom. The justices of the United States Supreme Court can change the law of the land. The inherent or perceived authority possessed by those in positions of power impact such declarations.

However, there is only one individual whose declarations are supported by "all authority in heaven and on earth." Because of that powerful link, Jesus' teachings are worthy of our attention and amazement. During this study of the Book of Mark, commit yourself to approach Jesus' teachings with a willing heart and an open mind. Prepare yourself to discover the truth that will "set you free" (John 8:32). Prepare yourself to be amazed!

Authority Prevails (1:23–24)

A good action movie always includes a dramatic clash between hero and villain. Such conflict is even more dramatic if the physical confrontation is set atop a moving train or on the pinnacle of a skyscraper. The setting depicted in Mark 1:23, a synagogue, did not lend itself to the dramatic. However, in that typically serene setting the authority of Jesus clashed with the demonic powers of hell. When two forces collide, the stronger one will rule. The result is the same during a confrontation of wills: a parent versus a strong-willed child; a teacher versus an unruly student; a citizen versus a bureaucracy. In Mark 1, Jesus boldly confronted an evil spirit, who cried, "What do you want with us, Jesus of Nazareth? Have you come to destroy us? (1:24). Jesus' reply was stern but simple. "Be quiet!"

This two-word reply was not a request; it was a command. Jesus did not allow the lesser authority to speak. He totally negated the evil spirit's influence. Both the demon and those within earshot had to submit to a greater authority.

We may not have such dramatic collisions with evil spirits, but lesser authorities are undoubtedly prevalent in our lives. Advertisements speak to us on a daily basis, telling us we need to purchase something that will make us better, smarter, slimmer, and happier. YouTube videos, Facebook posts, and other media leap from our smartphones, tablets, and laptops, clawing for our attention and allegiance. Lesser authorities speak into our lives and produce less than stellar results.

Can you identify the lesser authorities in your life? Have you allowed their influence to distract you from the authority of Jesus? How can you negate their influence? Is your will clashing with the authority of Christ? Remember, the greater authority will prevail.

Authority Produces Results (1:25–34)

Words have consequences. Proverbs 18:21 tells us, "The tongue has the power of life and death." Authoritative words are even more powerful. We know that Jesus' words were filled with power because they produced dramatic results. Jesus spoke and affected the natural—listeners in the synagogue. He also spoke and impacted the supernatural—evil spirits.

Jesus' simple, but direct command to the evil spirit was "Come out of him!" (1:25). Unable to resist the overwhelming power that it faced, the evil spirit departed with a shriek.

Jesus' words evoked a miracle. His absolute authority over the evil spirit was readily recognized and verbalized by all who observed the encounter: "He even gives orders to evil spirits and they obey him!" (1:27). Jesus' authority was unique, and news about him spread quickly. In today's social media terms, we would say his authority went viral. The hashtag #Jesuspower was trending!

The authority of Jesus also produced freedom and service. The man held captive by the evil spirit experienced the direct power of the authority of Jesus when freed from bondage. Simon's mother-in-law, afflicted in a different sense, also experienced freedom. Acts of service followed her freedom: "The fever left her and she began to wait on them" (1:31).

When you personally engage the authority of Jesus, your life will experience the impact of that authority in practical and visible ways. Have you seen the words of Jesus at work in your life?

But just how far could the authority of Jesus go? On that Sabbath day long ago, the people soon found out. After bringing "all the sick and demon-possessed" to Jesus, the "whole town" gathered near him (1:32–33). The result? Jesus healed "many" and drove out "many" demons (1:34). Jesus' authority met the needs of the people.

Are you afflicted on one level or another? Trust in the authority of the words of Jesus and his work. Does doubt keep you up at night? He will give you peace "which transcends all understanding" (Philippians 4:7). Is your body weary from illness? Jesus invites you, "Come to me, all you who are weary and burdened, and I will give you rest" (Matt. 11:28). Are financial challenges making you tense? He can "meet all your needs according to the riches of his glory in Christ Jesus" (Phil. 4:19).

Follow the example of the people who experienced the power of Jesus on that Sabbath day. Go to him. Experience his authority. It will produce dramatic results in your life.

Authority Serves and Transforms (1:35–39)

Authority can be intimidating. I remember an unexpected opportunity to eat breakfast with President Jimmy Carter. Unfortunately, I did not have much preparation time, and my phone did not have an application for presidential manners and procedures; however, I navigated that breakfast meeting without spilling coffee or offending the former leader of the free world.

Those with high authority may appear intimidating and less approachable. However, Jesus did not intimidate the people in the synagogue and the surrounding towns. Instead, they were drawn to him and his power. The disciples exclaimed, "Everyone is looking for you!" (1:37).

The people of Capernaum knew Jesus' teaching was different. He taught with authority that contrasted sharply with that of self-serving, divisive religious leaders and the tyrannical, prejudicial Roman authorities. Jesus had supreme authority which he used for a different purpose. "The Son of Man did not come to be served, but to serve, and to give his life as a ransom for many" (Matt. 20:28). Jesus was determined to share his life-changing authority with as many as would receive him.

Mark tells us that Jesus was ready to "go somewhere else" (Mark 1:38) and that he "traveled throughout Galilee, preaching in their synagogues and driving out demons" (1:39). Jesus made it clear why he was fervent about doing this: "This is why I have come" (1:38).

The authority of Jesus is available to you for freedom and healing. Are you willing to accept the authority of Jesus? That is why he came.

Implications and Actions

While he was on earth, Jesus made his authority clear to those around him. In his teaching, Jesus was distinct from other teachers in that his truths and principles exuded authority. When he encountered those afflicted by dark powers, such as unclean spirits, Jesus had the authority to set people free. Many who suffered illnesses experienced healing through Jesus' authority.

A natural tendency is to fear or flinch from authority. However, Jesus' authority drew people to him because of the love he displayed and his desire to use his authority to bless and transform people.

Think about how you have seen Jesus' authority play out in your life. Surrender the areas of your life that remain under the influence of lesser authorities. Invite Jesus to exert his authority in every part of your life.

The Power of Evil Spirits

Jesus demonstrated his authority during the encounter with an "evil spirit" (Mark 1:23). Let's examine a few passages in the Book of Mark to gain a better understanding of the type of power evil spirits exert.

Mark described evil spirits (demons) as visible and often destructive, able to:

- physically affect people (1:26)
- speak (1:24)
- cry out (1:26)
- inhabit animals (5:12)
- afflict both males (1:26) and females (7:26)

However, evil spirits are not invincible. Mark recorded that Jesus cast out demons (1:34, 6:13). Jesus also gave his disciples the power to cast out evil spirits (6:7). And, in his name, Jesus' followers could also cast them out (16:17).

Additionally, the Book of Mark gives clear evidence that those afflicted by evil spirits can be:

- set free (1:39), even when afflicted by multiple spirits (16:9)
- returned to a right state of mind (5:15)
- become followers of Jesus (5:18)

No matter what havoc demons wreck, Jesus' authority is superior.

Embrace the Authority of Jesus

Do you have an area in your life that you need to submit to the authority of Jesus? Consider these steps to freedom.

- Clearly define the affliction or need. Is it relational? Emotional? Is it the consequence of others' actions, your decisions, or something else?

- Find biblical truths that are relevant and applicable. Use the concordance in your Bible or do an online search for "Bible verses on _____" and fill-in the topic.
- Ask a mature believer to help you apply the Bible passages you discover.
- Daily read the passages and pray the truths, promises, or principles they reveal.

Questions

1. Can you recall your feelings the last time you confronted someone who has great authority?

2. Which of Jesus' teachings stands out as particularly authoritative?

3. What are some of the lesser authorities people regularly face?

4. What can you do to experience the power of Jesus working in your life?

5. What affliction are you facing that you would be willing to entrust to Jesus' authority today?

Notes

1. Unless otherwise indicated, all Scripture quotations in lessons 1–7 are from the New International Version (1984 edition).

lesson  2

Healing and Forgiveness

MAIN IDEA

Jesus revealed his identity by healing a paralytic and forgiving his sin.

QUESTION TO EXPLORE

What is the connection between faith and healing and forgiveness?

STUDY AIM

To lead adults to faithfully seek Jesus as their source for healing and forgiveness

QUICK READ

Jesus can pierce through the distractions of our lives and bring healing and forgiveness, often beyond our expectations.

Introduction

Who would turn down a fifty-cent lunch? Not hungry college students. That is why the two- quarter luncheon at the Baptist Student Ministry (BSM) was popular on my junior college campus. It was a great combination; students enjoyed an inexpensive home-cooked meal, and local pastors had a captive audience for a fifteen-minute devotional.

Well, almost captive. Students ate during the sermon, and they talked while they ate. Quick to return for seconds or dash to the next class, students constantly shuffled during the pastors' devotionals. It was after such an experience that one pastor told the BSM Director, "Don't invite me back. There's too much noise, and you need at least thirty minutes for a proper sermon!"

Can God work in a noisy crowd or when constrained to a fifteen-minute time frame? The Book of Mark reveals that Jesus preached to a rambunctious mass of people, bringing healing and forgiveness during imperfect circumstances.

Mark 2:1–12

1 A few days later, when Jesus again entered Capernaum, the people heard that he had come home. 2 So many gathered that there was no room left, not even outside the door, and he preached the word to them. 3 Some men came, bringing to him a paralytic, carried by four of them. 4 Since they could not get him to Jesus because of the crowd, they

made an opening in the roof above Jesus and, after digging through it, lowered the mat the paralyzed man was lying on. **5** When Jesus saw their faith, he said to the paralytic, "Son, your sins are forgiven."

6 Now some teachers of the law were sitting there, thinking to themselves, **7** "Why does this fellow talk like that? He's blaspheming! Who can forgive sins but God alone?"

8 Immediately Jesus knew in his spirit that this was what they were thinking in their hearts, and he said to them, "Why are you thinking these things? **9** Which is easier: to say to the paralytic, 'Your sins are forgiven,' or to say, 'Get up, take your mat and walk'? **10** But that you may know that the Son of Man has authority on earth to forgive sins. . . ." He said to the paralytic, **11** "I tell you, get up, take your mat and go home." **12** He got up, took his mat and walked out in full view of them all. This amazed everyone and they praised God, saying, "We have never seen anything like this!"

Christ in the Chaos of the Crowd (2:1–2)

Everyone was talking about Jesus. Since that first Sabbath when he spoke in the synagogue, everyone knew Jesus was different. He spoke with unbridled authority (1:22). He commanded demons, and they obeyed (1:25–26). He healed the sick, and not just once. "Jesus healed many . . . He also drove out many demons" (1:34).

Those feats garnered attention. A crowd gathered, combining those who were genuinely interested and others who simply wanted to be part of the conversation of the day.

Soon, more people arrived. Eventually, there were so many in the crowd "there was no room left, not even outside the door" (2:2).

A huge crowd is not the ideal setting for a one-on-one encounter. Consider the distractions. Undoubtedly, some in the crowd were genuinely interested and tried hard to hear Jesus as "he preached the word to them" (2:2). Others were carrying on side conversations: "Do we stay and listen or do you want to grab some dinner?" And surely there was a loud "shusher" in the crowd, more distracting than the background talking.

Then, there were sound barriers. Jesus was speaking from inside a home packed with people. Those outside the walls strained to hear his words.

Other communicators might have given up and delayed the event until there was a larger venue, better acoustics, and maybe even some crowd control. Other preachers might have given up trying to convey anything of value to the crowd.

But Jesus did not give up. He preached. In the chaos of the crowd, he preached. Knowing there were barriers between him and the listeners, he preached. Although acutely aware that some in the crowd were intent on creating distractions, Jesus preached. He did not allow those distractions to deter or defer his profound message.

Today, distractions bombard us. Is it hard for you to hear Jesus as you are surrounded by the chaos of the world? Work deadlines distract. Past hurts and things left undone divert attention, as do divisions. Is it hard to hear the words of

Jesus when the consequences of failure loom large? Do you feel pain so intense you cannot focus? Are you so preoccupied you have drifted out of listening range? Does the chasm of sin distance you from the Messiah?

You are not alone. Isaiah 59:2 speaks to all of us: "But your iniquities have separated you from your God; your sins have hidden his face from you, so that he will not hear."

Yet in the midst of the distance and the distraction, Jesus is still with you. He still speaks. He is speaking to you now amidst the chaos of life. Listen to him. He has "the words of eternal life" (John 6:68). Believe his words: "Whoever hears my word and believes him who sent me has eternal life" (John 5:24). The result will be abundant life in the chaos of the crowd.

What Faith Looks Like (2:3–5a)

It was a long shot, maybe their last shot. They had to take it. And, they had to take him. Carrying their paralyzed friend to Jesus was no easy task. They lost track of the times they had to stop along the way to put their friend down, adjust their grips on the makeshift gurney, and with a huge heave lift him again. Each time, their muscles quivered. Each time they walked a shorter distance before needing to rest. One of them kept his eyes focused on the ground, watching for obstacles, channeling his strength to the grip his hands had on his friend, only to finally look up to see an impenetrable barricade of bodies in front of the house where Jesus was staying.

Their only option was to go up. So, they hauled their friend to the roof, removed the roofing material, and with fading strength, lowered their friend in front of the man they had heard so much about.

When he looked at the paralyzed man's four friends, Jesus saw faith in their compassionate effort. Faith was visible in the beads of sweat that poured down their faces. Jesus saw faith in their hands, scraped and perhaps bleeding due to the strain of the ropes as they lowered their friend through the roof. Their faith revealed itself through perseverance when a barricade of bodies, a high roof, and a risky maneuver did not deter them from introducing their friend to Jesus Christ.

Can Jesus see your faith? If so, what does it look like?

Your faith is not limited to supernatural revelations. Others can see your faith when you "turn the other cheek" (Matthew 5:39). It is visible when you give your coat or a bottle of water to someone who is homeless (Mark 9:41). Your faith is evident when you go the extra mile (Matt. 5:41) and when you love those who treat you like dirt (Luke 6:27).

More often than not, faith is gritty and sweaty, its carriers bruised and exhausted.

And Jesus sees it.

The Easier of Two Impossible Things (2:5b–12)

Jesus had healed many. Would he do it again? The need was evident. Anticipation rippled the air. Would Jesus say the word and heal the paralyzed man right before their eyes?

Jesus spoke, but not the words everyone was expecting. "Son, your sins are forgiven" (2:5). A plethora of emotions ricocheted throughout the room at the sound of Jesus' words declaring forgiveness to the paralytic. The four friends, who had labored for a work of healing, not a spiritual proclamation, likely hung their heads through the roof hole confused and dismayed. Those who had waited for supernatural drama rather than another "sin talk" were woefully disappointed. And intense anger boiled in the hearts and minds of the teachers of the law. "Why does this fellow talk like that? He's blaspheming! Who can forgive sins but God alone?" (2:7).

The teachers of the law knew about God and his forgiveness. They knew their God was "merciful and forgiving" (Daniel 9:9). They knew their God as "he who blots out your transgressions . . . and remembers your sins no more" (Isaiah 43:25). But they questioned, "Who is a God like you, who pardons sin. . . ?" (Micah 7:18).

The teachers of the law made a correct declaration, but they missed the connection. They were right in declaring only God can forgive sins but failed to grasp that Jesus is God!

When God does not meet our expectations, we, too, can miss the connection. The teachers of the law were expecting a Messiah seated on a throne with the power to destroy oppressors and establish the reign of King David's heirs. When the Messiah appeared, born of a pure maiden, raised by a carpenter, and buddies with fishermen and tax collectors, such a resume did not meet the religious leaders' expectations.

The religious leaders were not expecting Jesus to make a declaration of forgiveness. Everyday people were expecting another dramatic miracle. Jesus failed to meet either expectation. Instead, he brought forgiveness to a heart and transformation to a life.

Jesus certainly had everyone's attention when the teachers of the law lambasted his declaration of forgiveness. So, no one missed his follow-up question: "Which is easier: to say to this paralyzed man, 'Your sins are forgiven,' or to say, 'Get up, take your mat and walk'?" (2:9). Both declarations were equally impossible—for a man. But for God? He had the power to do both.

And Jesus did both. In doing so, he revealed himself as God. "This amazed everyone and they praised God" (2:12).

The teachers had expected some new insight or twist on a spiritual teaching. The paralyzed man and his friends expected a physical transformation. Jesus provided both, and more.

Do your expectations of Christ remain unmet? Your religious tradition or personal experiences may limit your expectations of Jesus. "I have never seen Jesus do that." Or, "That's never happened to me." Maybe you expect Jesus to teach you something new, help you be a nicer person, or intrigue you with spiritual insight. Jesus can do, and wants to do, so much more than what you expect of him.

Jesus set the bar for what we should expect when we come to him. "I have come that they may have life, and have it to the full" (John 10:10). "Come to me," Jesus says, "all you who are weary and burdened, and I will give you rest" (Matt. 11:28). "You may ask me for anything in my name, and I will do it" (John 14:14). His assurance is "whoever comes to me I will never drive away" (John 6:37).

Whatever your expectations are of Jesus, they will always prove too low, too shallow, and too temporary. From now on, when you approach Jesus in prayer or worship, remember that he is "able to do immeasurably more than all we ask or imagine" (Ephesians 3:20).

When we allow Jesus to forgive us and to heal us, we too will say, "We have never seen anything like this!" (Mark 2:12).

Implications and Actions

All too often, our needs remain far removed from Jesus, the source of healing and forgiveness. However, Jesus remains undistracted by the distractions that separate us from him. He is undeterred by deterrents that act to keep us distant from him. He remains accessible.

While four friends physically carried the paralyzed man, it was their faith that brought him to the feet of Jesus. And it is faith that leads us to Jesus. Jesus saw the men's faith in their actions. Likewise, Jesus will see our faith as we strive to bring others to him.

Jesus is ready to exceed our expectations of him. His forgiveness and healing are available to do their work in us. Just like the men the Book of Mark describes, we need to approach Jesus in faith.

A Few Words About Blasphemy

"He's blaspheming!" declared the teachers of the law when they heard Jesus say, "Son, your sins are forgiven" (Mark 2:5–7). Blasphemy is often defined as the slander or defamation of God or the taking on of the attributes of God. The Book of Mark records that claiming to forgive sins certainly met the religious leaders' definition of blasphemy.

In Matthew 26:65, Jesus' claim to be God was declared blasphemous by the high priest. It was so offensive to the prevailing religious understanding of the day that the high priest ripped his clothes, and the chief priests said, "He is worthy of death" (26:66).

Similarly, in John 10:30, Jesus declared, "I and the Father are one." The Jewish opponents responded, "We are not stoning you for any good work . . . but for blasphemy, because you, a mere man, claim to be God" (10:33).

The Jewish leaders were certainly zealous in their protection of God's name and reputation. So much so, they failed to see God in Jesus Christ.

Case Study

Marshall has several things working against him. His job often requires him to work on days that keep him from regularly attending church or Bible study. There are things in his personal life that distract him from experiencing spiritual growth. What are two or three practical things you could do to help bring Marshall closer to connecting with Jesus?

Questions

1. Has there been a time in your life when Jesus appeared beyond reach?

2. How has someone helped you draw closer to Jesus?

3. Do you remember a time when God did something that far exceeded your expectations?

4. What have you done that enabled people to see your faith?

lesson 3

A Case of Mistaken Identity

MAIN IDEA

Jesus' family and religious leaders from Jerusalem failed to recognize his identity and mission.

QUESTION TO EXPLORE

How should we respond to attacks and insinuations from others, including family members?

STUDY AIM

To become convinced that embracing Jesus and his mission must be my priority

QUICK READ

Jesus' family failed to recognize his mission while the teachers of the law failed to recognize the power of the Spirit. In this lesson, we learn to embrace both.

Introduction

"Have you joined a cult?" That was the question friends were asking a married couple who had begun attending our church. They had made dramatic lifestyle changes based on newly embraced biblical principles. The way the couple handled their finances dramatically changed. Previously they accepted every dinner and movie invitation. Now, they were more conscientious about their entertainment choices. Previously, whether they had the money or not, the two were always buying stuff. Now, they exercised discipline in their spending. The changes in their lives were so evident, and the couple's commitment so cemented, friends no longer recognized the pair.

Interestingly enough, the family of Jesus experienced a similar identity crisis. After thirty years, the Jesus they grew up with was saying and doing unusual things. They questioned his identity—and his sanity. In the middle of this family crisis, Jesus revealed his true identity and why he came to the world.

The passage in this lesson will help you recognize Jesus' identity and mission so you can embrace it and make it your own.

Mark 3:20–35

20 Then Jesus entered a house, and again a crowd gathered, so that he and his disciples were not even able to

46

eat. **21** When his family heard about this, they went to take charge of him, for they said, "He is out of his mind."

22 And the teachers of the law who came down from Jerusalem said, "He is possessed by Beelzebub! By the prince of demons he is driving out demons."

23 So Jesus called them and spoke to them in parables: "How can Satan drive out Satan?**24** If a kingdom is divided against itself, that kingdom cannot stand. **25** If a house is divided against itself, that house cannot stand. **26** And if Satan opposes himself and is divided, he cannot stand; his end has come. **27** In fact, no one can enter a strong man's house and carry off his possessions unless he first ties up the strong man. Then he can rob his house. **28** I tell you the truth, all the sins and blasphemies of men will be forgiven them. **29** But whoever blasphemes against the Holy Spirit will never be forgiven; he is guilty of an eternal sin."

30 He said this because they were saying, "He has an evil spirit."

31 Then Jesus' mother and brothers arrived. Standing outside, they sent someone in to call him. **32** A crowd was sitting around him, and they told him, "Your mother and brothers are outside looking for you."

33 "Who are my mother and my brothers?" he asked.

34 Then he looked at those seated in a circle around him and said, "Here are my mother and my brothers! **35** Whoever does God's will is my brother and sister and mother."

The Rogue Family Member (3:20–21)

It could not have been easy growing up with the Son of God as a family member. He never disobeyed his parents. He always told the truth. He was perpetually kind, worked hard, and always did more than he was asked to do. He was different. He did not look at the world the way others did.

But the family secret was out. It was one thing for Jesus to talk about his radical beliefs around the family dinner table. It was quite another to do so in the synagogue, in the homes of friends, and in the public square. People were paying attention. Every day more of them asked the question, *Who does this son of a carpenter think he is?*

Jesus soon answered that question. "Then Jesus entered a house, and again a crowd gathered." (3:20). It was one thing for Jesus to put his personal reputation on the line, but placing the family name at risk was a different matter. Jesus needing reining in, and his family decided it was up to them to do the job. "They went to take charge of him, for they said, 'He is out of his mind'" (3:21).

Has Jesus ever gotten out of control in your life? Sure, it was okay at the beginning when he forgave your sins. What a relief! Then Jesus walked out of the privacy of the personal and began to make public appearances. He wanted to guide your relationships. He wanted to change the way you treated your co-workers and even the way you work. He wanted to restructure your finances and harness your tongue, maybe even change your professional plans and lifelong dreams.

You may hesitate to say, "Jesus is out of his mind." But perhaps your thought process sounds like this: *He is out of his jurisdiction. We are talking about my professional life, not a church service. That money is my quarterly bonus, not an offering for the poor.*

Much like the immediate family of Jesus, perhaps you have tried to "take charge of him." Have you attempted to haul Jesus back into the area of your life known as "church" or "spirituality." Do you sometimes act as if Jesus has gone too far in your life?

Stop for a moment and think about what would happen if the person and power of Jesus had free reign in every area of your life. Instead of reining him in, let Jesus reign.

Family Ties (3:31–34)

Before Jesus' family arrived on the scene, he and the teachers of the law had a dramatic confrontation. (See the sidebar "Intercalations.") Then, Jesus got the message that his mother and brothers wanted to speak with him outside (3:32). Jesus responded, "Who are my mother and my brothers?" (3:33). Looking at the people around him, he said, "Here are my mother and my brothers!" (3:34).

No, Jesus was not experiencing a sudden bout of amnesia regarding his family relationships. Family relationships were at the core of Jewish society. One did not disown family on a whim. Jesus' question and his odd declaration regarding his family would have stunned his Jewish listeners.

Jesus seized the moment to use the familiar to express the unfamiliar. "Whoever does God's will is my brother and sister and mother" (3:35). The listeners understood the concept of family and physical relationships, but Jesus introduced a new type of relationship, one not dependent on bloodlines or parentage.

This new relationship existed on another level and was of a different breadth. Jesus spoke of a spiritual relationship, one based on a shared spiritual Father, rather than a shared human father. Belonging to a human family was limited by geography, time, social position, and a myriad of other binding factors. Jesus declared no such limitations when it came to having a relationship with him. It was open to anyone: "There is neither Jew nor Greek, slave nor free, male nor female, for you are all one in Christ Jesus" (Galatians 3:28). A relationship with Jesus, through the Holy Spirit, was available to all in spite of time and distance: "The promise is for you and your children and for all who are far off—for all whom the Lord our God will call" (Acts 2:39).

You can connect directly with Jesus and be part of his family. God himself has given you the right to become a child of God, all you have to do is receive him and believe in his name (John 1:12).

If you are already a part of God's family, do not let earthly family shortcomings distract you from the joy of belonging to God's family. "How great is the love the Father has lavished on us, that we should be called children of God! And that is what we are!" (1 John 3:1). Make it a practice to celebrate some quality family time.

Irresponsible Positions and Irrevocable Decisions (3:22–30)

His family and the crowds were not the only ones who noticed Jesus. The teachers of the law were increasingly suspicious and jealous of the influence Jesus garnered as he taught and healed, so they confronted him. Their accusations were quick and vicious. They did not challenge that Jesus had performed a miracle by casting out demons. They challenged how he had accomplished the feat. The teachers of the law ascribed the work to the devil. They refused to recognize the power of the Spirit at work.

Jesus did not flinch or retreat. "Jesus called them over to him and began to speak to them in parables" (3:23). To show them the impossibility of their accusation, Jesus addressed their erroneous argument from two logical perspectives.

First, Jesus spoke to the fallacy of their premise, "by the prince of demons he is driving out demons" (3:22). Jesus' simple response was "How can Satan drive out Satan?" (3:23). It was ludicrous to claim that Satan was kicking himself out of those who were demon-possessed. To make it even clearer, Jesus illustrated that neither a kingdom nor a house, not even Satan, can self-attack and remain standing (3:24–26).

Second, when the teachers of the law ignored logical, rudimentary spiritual principles of good and evil, Jesus brought things down to earth: "In fact, no one can enter a strong man's house and carry off his possessions unless he first ties up the strong man. Then he can rob his house" (3:27). If the demons were cast out by the power of Satan, then the devil himself would have had to enter the demon-possessed and tie himself up to plunder himself.

Jesus concluded his response to the allegations by reminding the teachers of the law that God will forgive all the sins of men "but whoever blasphemes against the Holy Spirit will never be forgiven; he is guilty of an eternal sin" (3:28–29). Like many statements of Jesus, this one has caused consternation both to those in theological discussions and to those who fear being guilty of the eternal sin. Understanding the unpardonable sin is aided by the subsequent verse that states why Jesus mentioned the eternal sin. "He said this because they said, 'He has an impure spirit'" (3:30). Note that the word *elegon* – translated as "were saying" – is used in the imperfect sense. This indicates a continuous action. In other words, this was not just something the teachers of the law blurted out. It was an incessant accusation.

Their persistent claim that Satan, rather than the Spirit, was the source of the miracles of Jesus, was indicative of the condition of their souls. "You brood of vipers, how can you who are evil say anything good? For the mouth speaks what the heart is full of" (Matthew 12:34). When someone deliberately persists in rejecting the work of the Spirit, he or she runs the risk that death makes their choice irrevocable, and thus, it becomes the final and eternal state of their soul.

There may be some who are worried about being guilty of blaspheming the Holy Spirit and think that forgiveness is no longer available to them. However, remember what Jesus said about the Holy Spirit's mission: "He will convict the world concerning sin . . . because they do not believe in Me" (John 16:8–9, NASB).

If you feel conviction about sin and the state of your soul, it is because the Holy Spirit is at work in you. Respond to the Spirit. Receive the Spirit. The Spirit will give you life (Romans 8:11) and give you the assurance that God abides in you (1 John 3:24; 4:13).

Implications and Actions

Although Jesus' family had embraced him, they initially did not embrace his mission. Jesus' powerful miracles, growing following, and counter-cultural teachings were part of his God-given mission. These actions also led Jesus' family to declare him mentally unstable. Jesus stretched their understanding of family and relationships by stating that anyone who did his Father's (God's) will would be part of Jesus' family.

How will you fully embrace Jesus, his mission, and the Father's will? Jesus did it by sharing life-changing truths, bringing restoration and healing to the aggrieved, and freedom to the oppressed. Whether at work or home, as a volunteer or employee, around the block or around the world, or on social media; you can do the same.

The Sandwich Writing Style

Intercalation is the word Bible scholars use to describe the practice of an author splitting one story by inserting a second story between the beginning and ending of the first one. Sometimes this technique is called ABA style, where A represents the first story and B the second. This approach leads some to refer to it as the "sandwich" writing style.

In addition to the key passage in today's lesson, Mark employed the intercalation literary technique several times throughout his Gospel. Examine the following intercalations and determine how the inserted story relates to the initial story.

- Mark 5:21–43: Jesus healed the daughter of Jairus—and the woman with the issue of blood.

- Mark 6:7–34: Jesus sent the twelve disciples to spread the gospel—and John the Baptist was beheaded.

- Mark 11:12–14: Jesus cursed a fig tree—and he overturned the temple tables.

- Mark 14:1–11: The high priest and Judas plotted to catch Jesus—and a woman anointed Jesus.

- Mark 14:54–72: Peter sat near the fire and denied Jesus—and Jesus stood before the high priest.

Case Study

Lately, Jim has been having disturbing thoughts. He constantly reviews the faults and failures of his life. He cannot get over the grievous sins he has committed. He has prayed, read the Bible and goes to the church altar for prayer every Sunday. He is not sure whether God is trying to tell him something about his sin, or if it is Satan reminding him of his past. How might you help Jim gain a healthy understanding of sin, conviction, and forgiveness?

Questions

1. What are some things others see Christians doing that may cause them to question the sanity of Christ-followers?

2. How is your spiritual family similar to your natural family? How is it different?

ON YOUR MARK: THE GOSPEL IN MOTION

3. What are some things people might try to do to "take charge" of Jesus and his work in them?

4. What evidence indicates that someone has embraced Jesus' mission and made it a priority in his or her life? Is this evident in your life?

lesson  4

Invading the Darkness

MAIN IDEA

Jesus revealed his power to a darkened land and a demon-possessed man.

QUESTION TO EXPLORE

How willing are we to confront the darkness in our world?

STUDY AIM

To choose to confront the darkness in the world with the power of Jesus

QUICK READ

Mark shows us that the works of darkness are real, and their effects are devastating. Fortunately, the transformational power of Jesus yields amazing results.

Introduction

The disciples most likely did not know it, but what they were about to experience on a lake that night was a preamble to, and preparation for, an even more unique experience to follow.

Their day had begun like a grand Bible study by the lake. Jesus shared the Parable of the Sower, talked about a light on a stand, and described the kingdom of God as a growing seed and a mustard plant (Mark 4:1–34). As evening neared, Jesus instructed his disciples to go to the other side of the lake. As the winds gained speed and the waves began to splash over the boats, an easy trip across the lake soon became dangerous.

In the middle of it all, Jesus slept. Waking him, the disciples asked, "Teacher, don't you care if we drown?" (4:38). With a quick rebuke to the wind and waves, Jesus commanded "Quiet! Be still!" and the lake was suddenly calm (4:39). Then, Jesus had a question for them: "Why are you so afraid? Do you still have no faith?" (4:40). In their terrified state, all they could answer was "Who is this? Even the wind and the waves obey him!" (4:41).

As the Book of Mark reveals, Jesus regularly demonstrated his power and authority. However, this time, Jesus' demonstration of power was over nature, and nature itself submitted to Jesus' authority.

Jesus knew he had to prepare the disciples to engage their fears with faith because a situation brooding with fear was waiting on the other side of the lake.

Mark 5:1–20

1 They went across the lake to the region of the Gerasenes. **2** When Jesus got out of the boat, a man with an evil spirit came from the tombs to meet him. **3** This man lived in the tombs, and no one could bind him any more, not even with a chain. **4** For he had often been chained hand and foot, but he tore the chains apart and broke the irons on his feet. No one was strong enough to subdue him. **5** Night and day among the tombs and in the hills he would cry out and cut himself with stones.

6 When he saw Jesus from a distance, he ran and fell on his knees in front of him. **7** He shouted at the top of his voice, "What do you want with me, Jesus, Son of the Most High God? Swear to God that you won't torture me!" **8** For Jesus had said to him, "Come out of this man, you evil spirit!"

9 Then Jesus asked him, "What is your name?" **10** "My name is Legion," he replied, "for we are many." And he begged Jesus again and again not to send them out of the area.

11 A large herd of pigs was feeding on the nearby hillside. **12** The demons begged Jesus, "Send us among the pigs; allow us to go into them." **13** He gave them permission, and the evil spirits came out and went into the pigs. The herd, about two thousand in number, rushed down the steep bank into the lake and were drowned.

[14] Those tending the pigs ran off and reported this in the town and countryside, and the people went out to see what had happened. [15] When they came to Jesus, they saw the man who had been possessed by the legion of demons, sitting there, dressed and in his right mind; and they were afraid. [16] Those who had seen it told the people what had happened to the demon-possessed man—and told about the pigs as well. [17] Then the people began to plead with Jesus to leave their region.

[18] As Jesus was getting into the boat, the man who had been demon-possessed begged to go with him. [19] Jesus did not let him, but said, "Go home to your family and tell them how much the Lord has done for you, and how he has had mercy on you." [20] So the man went away and began to tell in the Decapolis how much Jesus had done for him. And all the people were amazed.

What Darkness Does Well (5:1–2)

A man with an evil spirit came to meet Jesus and the disciples as they got off the boat (5:2). The evil spirit had done quite a devastating work in the man's life, ultimately leading him to live his days among the tombs. He was not the welcoming committee the disciples expected.

Home is a place for family, relationships, community, and fellowship. Think birthday parties, *quinceañeras*, and backyard cookouts. At home, life and love are shared.

Nothing is more antithetical to home than a cemetery. Due to the separation caused by death, a graveyard is a reminder of absent relationships and broken community. People mourn among the headstones, which symbolize life lost. The demoniac's existence is a reminder to us of what darkness does so well. Satan's work in our lives moves us from the land of the living to the land of the lifeless.

Is there an area of your life where darkness is beginning to abide? Perhaps sin's dark shadow has started to spread, bringing broken relationships, isolation, and self-destructive actions.

Admitting that darkness has cast its shade in our lives is the beginning of victory over it. The next step is confessing any role we have played in letting darkness do its thing. Ultimately, we share the demoniac's hope as our only hope: the power of Jesus.

Destruction Empowered (5:3–5)

The work of darkness in the demoniac was a threat to those around him. All restraints used to bind the man, even chains, failed. "He had often been chained hand and foot, but he tore the chains apart and broke the irons on his feet" (5:4). The demons empowered the man they inhabited. However, the dark power at work in him served only one purpose—his destruction.

Many things in this world can make us feel empowered, including an earned title, money amassed, or influence gained. Such empowerments enable us to accomplish new things. However, we must guard against power that leads to ruin. Access to power is useless if it is opposed to God's purposes.

People wanted to help the demon-possessed man whose life was a living terror, but "no one was strong enough to subdue him" (5:4). The powers of darkness defeated every contender. However, that day by the lake, the dark side met its match. Jesus confronted the darkness head-on.

Can you think of something in your life, maybe even something good, that is working against you? What was originally a benefit has begun to hurt your relationships, drain your faith, and cause problems at home or work. That something does not have to be demonic to cause loss and havoc. Examine your life to discover anything that has begun to tear down, rather than build up God's good work in you. Give it over to Jesus today.

The torment produced by the powers of darkness was evident in the daily existence of the man with the evil spirit. "Night and day among the tombs and in the hills he would cry out" (5:5). The Gerasene knew he needed help. His desperation was evident, and so was his self-destruction. Self-mutilation with stones further exasperated the man's affliction.

Demons and cemetery-living aside, the self-destructive work of darkness is all too common today. The scale and breadth may be different; however, the effects are no less painful. The unending torment of bullying endured daily by children can make school unbearable and learning next to impossible. When a father explodes with a regular barrage of verbal and emotional abuse, his wife and children are forced to endure a miserable existence. Turn to the issues of human trafficking, prostitution, and dictatorial regimes, and the destruction and suffering quickly escalate to an unimaginable scale.

Darkness is hard at work. So is Jesus. "The light shines in the darkness, and the darkness has not understood it" (John 1:5). Zechariah prophesied that Jesus would come "to shine on those living in darkness and in the shadow of death, to guide our feet into the path of peace" (Luke 1:79).

If you are suffering pain or destruction because of sin or the work of darkness, take heart. Jesus' death overcame Satan's work to "break the power of him who holds the power of death – that is, the devil" (Hebrews 2:14). The light of Christ is here, and darkness cannot overcome it. Jesus is ready to guide the hurting heart to the path of peace.

Deliverance Experienced (5:6–20)

We must give the evil spirit who possessed the Gerasene credit where credit is due; it recognized power and authority. Not as an act of worship, but as an act of submission, the man fell on his knees in front of Jesus (5:6). Jesus commanded the evil spirit to leave. The demon spoke through the man, and his words reveal the awareness of the person and position of Jesus: "What do you want with me, Jesus, Son of the Most High God?" (5:7). The words also acknowledged who had the upper hand in this confrontation, "Swear to God that you won't torture me!" (5:7).

Jesus asked the demon to identify itself, even though the omniscient Christ knew exactly with whom he was dealing. The identification was for the fearful and confused people who did not know the extent of the darkness that was at work in their midst. "My name is Legion," he replied, "for we are many" (5:9). All demons must submit to the power of Jesus.

The demons asked Jesus not to send them away because they wanted to remain nearby (5:10). Finding what they perceived as a viable alternative, the demons begged Jesus to allow them to enter a large herd of about 2,000 pigs feeding on the nearby hillside (5:11–12). Jesus granted permission, and the demons entered the herd. In a turn that the demons did not anticipate, the pigs rushed down a steep bank into the lake and drowned (5:13).

We could surmise about why the demons did not want to leave the area and guess as to why Jesus granted the request. We can even argue about why Jesus' work involved the death of so many animals. The results, however, are not debatable.

It was clear that Jesus' work in the man produced a change in his person. It yielded self-control: "When they came to Jesus, they saw the man who had been possessed by the legion of demons, sitting there" (5:15). Jesus restored the man's dignity and honor; he was "dressed." The freedom the man received from Jesus put him "in his right mind" (5:15).

Jesus also changed the man's purpose. The Gerasene abandoned the tombstones and "begged to go" with Jesus (5:18). Instead, Jesus made him a missionary right where he lived.

Jesus' instructions were precise. "Go home to your own people and tell them how much the Lord has done for you, and how he has had mercy on you" (5:19). The man's family and neighbors had witnessed the intense pain and destruction the demons had caused the Gerasene. As a result, they would have the greatest appreciation for Jesus' liberating work in the man's life.

Who has seen you at your worst? Who was there during the darkest time in your life? Have you shared with those people what Jesus has done for you?

Pray about letting these people know about your personal transformation that has been brought about by the power of Christ. When you share with them, you may get the same response the Gerasene received. "All the people were amazed" (5:20).

Implications and Actions

Jesus' encounter with the demon-possessed man demonstrates that dark, demonic powers are real. They can affect people physically, mentally, emotionally, and spiritually. These forces can even work to empower the destruction of individuals.

The damaging influence of darkness is just as real today as it was during the lifetime of the Gerasene man. However, just as Jesus revealed the power of demons, he also demonstrated the power of his Spirit to bring freedom and restoration. The teachers of the law refused to acknowledge the Spirit's power to deliver and brought upon themselves damning spiritual risk. The demoniac experienced the transformative power of Jesus.

Jesus' power is available today to those willing to allow it to work in them.

Understanding the "Unclean"

The theme of uncleanness is prevalent in Mark 5. The Greek word *akathartos* is translated as *impure* or *unclean* when describing the spirit of the Gerasene man (5:2). The word can refer to uncleanness in a ceremonial sense. The Levitical law declared many things unclean.

In the Mark 5 passage, the spirit is described as unclean. Corpses filled the demoniac's adopted home, and contact with a dead body made one unclean (Numbers 5:2, 19:11). The pig was an unclean animal (Leviticus 11:7). The Levitical law dictated Jews could not eat pig meat, and a pig carcass could not be touched (Lev. 11:8). Jews were commanded not to defile themselves by eating unclean animals (Lev. 20:25–26). Mark goes to the extent of noting that there were "about two thousand" of these unclean animals on the scene of Jesus' miracle (Mark 5:13).

In the midst of so much uncleanness, the power of Jesus prevailed. Whatever our surroundings or sins, we must remember that "the blood of Jesus his Son cleanses us" (1 John 1:7 NASB), and "he is faithful and just and will forgive us our sins and purify us" (1 John 1:9 NIV).

Case Study

Sarah was intrigued by a movie she saw that had a strong occult theme. After researching the occult on the Internet, her interest was piqued even more. Soon, she was experimenting with tarot cards, Ouija boards, and more. She has begun to have a constant uneasiness accompanied by nervousness that she cannot explain. Nightmares have become more regular, and fear is now a regular part of her life. She has come to you for help. What should you do?

Questions

1. Have you witnessed the powers of darkness at work in someone's life? What have you seen?

2. What are some things that give people power but can also hurt them?

3. If Jesus were to send you as a missionary to those who know you best, where would he send you?

4. What is something you have seen Jesus do in someone's life that left you amazed?

lesson 5

Rejection and Replication

MAIN IDEA

Jesus was rejected by his hometown and sent his disciples to replicate his ministry.

QUESTION TO EXPLORE

How have your preconceived notions prevented God from working in and through your life?

STUDY AIM

To evaluate my preconceived notions about God and to choose to follow him in simple obedience

QUICK READ

The Nazarenes' expectations of Jesus limited his opportunities to minister to them. May we learn from their mistakes, believe God keeps his promises, and walk in obedience, even in difficulty.

Introduction

My great Aunt Mable did not want me to grow up.[1] Every year when I visited her, she would look at me, and say, "The last time I saw you, you were this big," motioning to a spot at her waistline. In her mind, I remained the little girl she held as she read to me. Aunt Mable had preconceptions she struggled to alter.

Jesus knew people like my Aunt Mable. Those in his hometown viewed him with incomplete understanding and misconception. They responded to him with shallow assumptions and prejudice, surmising his background and family tree could not result in an adulthood of value and influence. As a result, the townspeople of Nazareth missed out on blessings. When we try to fit Christ into our preconceptions, we do not act in full obedience to his commands, and we miss out on blessings.

Mark 6:1–13

[1] Jesus left there and went to his hometown, accompanied by his disciples. [2] When the Sabbath came, he began to teach in the synagogue, and many who heard him were amazed.

"Where did this man get these things?" they asked. "What's this wisdom that has been given him, that he even does miracles! [3] Isn't this the carpenter? Isn't this Mary's son and the brother of James, Joseph, Judas and Simon? Aren't his sisters here with us?" And they took offense at him.

4 Jesus said to them, "Only in his hometown, among his relatives and in his own house is a prophet without honor." **5** He could not do any miracles there, except lay his hands on a few sick people and heal them. **6** And he was amazed at their lack of faith.

Then Jesus went around teaching from village to village. **7** Calling the Twelve to him, he sent them out two by two and gave them authority over evil spirits.

8 These were his instructions: "Take nothing for the journey except a staff—no bread, no bag, no money in your belts. **9** Wear sandals but not an extra tunic. **10** Whenever you enter a house, stay there until you leave that town. **11** And if any place will not welcome you or listen to you, shake the dust off your feet when you leave, as a testimony against them."

12 They went out and preached that people should repent. **13** They drove out many demons and anointed many sick people with oil and healed them.

There's No Place Like Home and Sometimes That Is a Good Thing (6:1–6)

After healing a sick woman who merely touched the hem of his garment and raising the daughter of Jairus from the dead because of the man's faith (Mark 5:22–43), Jesus returned home, traveling southwest from the Sea of Galilee's western shore toward his family in Nazareth. With the proliferation of miracles he was performing, curiosity was piqued, crowds were growing, word about Jesus was spreading, and expectations were rising—except in his hometown. While miracles occurred in other regions as the result of steadfast faith, Mark 6 contrasts the stark absence of faith found in Nazareth.

The Twelve knew Jesus as their rabbi (teacher), and he entered the small community of Nazareth as an instructor (6:1). However, the Nazarenes simply perceived him as a son returning home. They expected Jesus to meet their old, familiar expectations as the son of Mary and her husband Joseph, the carpenter.

Customarily, synagogue leaders gave visiting rabbis the opportunity to teach from the Law or Prophets on the Sabbath. With his entourage of disciples and the crowds that followed him, Jesus was clearly a rabbi, although the townspeople knew his background, and doubted his qualifications or capabilities. In fact, his family questioned Jesus' mental stability (3:21). Nevertheless, Jesus took the opportunity to teach (6:2).[2] More than likely, it was the first time Nazarenes heard Jesus preach, and they were "amazed" (Greek word *ekplesso* means surprised and incredulous).

In light of their preconceptions of Jesus, his teaching was more than they could comprehend, and their astonishment rapidly declined into suspicion. Imagine the squinting eyes and shocked expressions of the townspeople. Whispers edged with skepticism likely became louder the longer Jesus spoke. "Where did this man get these things?" they asked. "What's this wisdom that has been given him?" (6:2).

These questions were not authentic searches for answers; they were curt and tactless sarcasm. How could one so familiar to them possess such wisdom? And though there is no record of Jesus performing miracles in Nazareth, rumors of his marvelous acts had apparently traveled there. Instead of asking, *"What does this mean? Why is he able to do these things?"* the villagers were more interested in confirming "their private prejudice that he [could not] be all that remarkable."[3] After all, he was a carpenter, and everyone knew his background and immediate family (6:3). (See the sidebar "Jesus the Carpenter?")

There was nothing extraordinary about his family, so why would Jesus be something special? The villagers perceived him as a common, ordinary fellow who made his living with his hands (like most of them), not as one with a capacity for greatness. *How dare he have the audacity to speak with such authority? Only someone prominently born could be an extraordinary leader or demonstrate such competence with Scripture!*

The villagers' comments about Mary reflected disdain. In a patriarchal society, it was derogatory for someone to describe a grown man as his mother's son. Perhaps this designation indicated the unceasing rumors of his illegitimacy; gossip that tagged Jesus throughout his lifetime. The siblings mentioned by the villagers were indeed half-brothers and sisters of Jesus, Mary and Joseph's children. (See the sidebar "We Are Family.")

Since the Nazarenes could not come to terms with what they observed, they "took offense" (Greek word *skandalizomai;* cf. Romans 9:33; 1 Corinthians 1:23). This verb, from which is derived the English word *scandal*, connotes deep denial and rejection leading to abandonment. The people of Nazareth refused to accept Jesus for what they saw from him and certainly did not view him as their long-awaited Messiah. It was as if they believed nothing this good could come from their hometown (John 1:46)![4] It is unclear whether the villagers verbalized their displeasure directly to Jesus. Nevertheless, he knew their hearts, and responded with a proverb familiar to them (6:4); a proven truth since even his family, those who lived with him and knew him best, rejected him for a while (John 7:5).

Because of the profound unbelief present in Nazareth, Jesus imposed personal limitations on his ministry. He was not interested in impressing his hometown with miracles. Instead, he was committed to obedience to his Heavenly Father (John 8:28; 14:31). John 10:38 makes this clear: "But if I do it, even though you do not believe me, believe the miracles, that you may know and understand that the Father is in me, and I in the Father."

If the people who watched Jesus grow from childhood could not accept him as a rabbi or prophet, how would they ever believe he was God's Son? Throughout the Gospel of Mark, people were amazed at Jesus (1:27; 2:12; 5:20; 6:51; 10:24; 11:18; 12:17; 15:5); only in Nazareth was Jesus amazed at people, precisely at their lack of faith. Thus, Jesus left Nazareth and went to other villages to teach (6:5–6). We have no indication he ever returned to his hometown.

Do Not Expect It to Be Easy (6:7–13)

Jesus called the Twelve to "follow" him (Mark 1:17, 2:14), so in obedience, they walked with him wherever he led, absorbing his teaching, observing his behaviors, and aspiring to imitate him. In his wisdom, Jesus allowed them to see his rejection in Nazareth. In so doing, he prepared the disciples for rejection as he expanded their purpose and his sphere of influence through them. The Greek text implies Jesus sent them as his official representatives or delegates to fulfill the purposes for which he called them, as seen in Mark 3:14–15: "to preach and to have authority to drive out demons."[5]

Following customary Jewish practice, the disciples went out in pairs (6:7) for three apparent reasons: (1) to establish the truthfulness of their testimony about Jesus (cf. Numbers 35:30 and Deuteronomy 17:6; 19:15 where in legal matters two witnesses established evidence); (2) to decrease the temptation to be the center of attention, since they must work in tandem; and (3) for personal safety and emotional support.[6] Mark used the imperfect tense "gave them authority" (Greek *edidou*), which means Jesus kept on giving them a continuous power throughout their journeys, an important distinction and help for the task of exorcising demons, since "our struggle is not against flesh and blood" (Ephesians 6:12).

Surprisingly, rather than instruct his disciples on what to preach or do when they encountered demons, Jesus focused on what they should not pack (6:8–9). His men were to trust

God to provide hosts to meet their physical needs. They were not to take food but to believe God would provide it. They were not to carry a traveling bag or a beggar's bag since they were trusting God's provision.

They were not to take money (Greek *chalkos*, which was the smallest copper coin), nor an extra shirt, sometimes translated "cloak" or "tunic" even though it would have offered warmth, especially if they had to sleep outdoors. The minimum he allotted them—sandals and staff (walking stick)—protected their feet and steadied their steps. Jesus' desire was to restrict luxury. The limitations he set revealed the urgency of the disciples' mission; too many material things would load them down, slowing their efforts.

As we accumulate stuff, we become more self-reliant, convincing ourselves we are providing for our needs. Material things can limit our dependency on God, limit our connection with others instead of depending on their kindness, shackle us to selfishness, and may even hinder our obedience.

Next, Jesus addressed the behavior of the disciples during their mission. In the ancient world, religious philosophers went from house to house, looking for something bigger and better. If a guest left one host home for another, the original host was shamed in the community's eyes. Pagan philosophers did not care about that repercussion; but Jesus did. To contrast themselves from such practices and preserve an honorable reputation for themselves and their hosts, Jesus told his disciples to stay in one house (6:10) when welcomed. To do so revealed their priorities and an element of satisfaction and contentment about their circumstances, not a pickiness or lack of gratitude (cf. Paul in Philippians 4:10–12).

Jesus was honest about the challenge he placed before the Twelve. He knew they would be rejected at times, just as he was in Nazareth. Nevertheless, when this happened, Jesus instructed them to "shake the dust off your feet" (6:11). This practice was a custom performed by Jews before re-entering the Holy Land, believing the mere dust of pagan places could defile their homeland, so they carefully removed it from themselves. Practicing this as Jesus' disciples meant not wasting time with those who refused to listen, and declaring the place as heathen while issuing a warning concerning their likely omission from God's kingdom.

Obediently leaving Jesus, the disciples actively shared in his ministry, preaching repentance (6:12), casting out demons, and healing people as they anointed them with oil, a symbol of God's presence, grace and power (6:13). The only report we have of their work appears in Mark 6:30: "The apostles gathered around Jesus and reported to him all they had done and taught." This single report indicates Mark wanted the emphasis placed not on the results, which must be left in God's hands, but rather on God's proven faithfulness and the faith, self-sacrifice, and commitment it took to be obedient, even in the face of difficulty and rejection.

Implications and Actions

Mark frequently emphasized the importance of faith. The Nazarenes' lack of faith and their inability to overcome their preconceptions of Jesus limited his ministry to them. Faith was (and is) the critical link in a relationship with Christ because faith is not the result of miracles; it is a personal choice to believe based on careful examination of the facts. Jesus did not feel the need to convince the unbelieving with marvelous acts; he knew preconceptions were blocking the way for faith even while he taught with authority. Had the villagers of Nazareth had open minds, refusing to limit God, there may have been enough of a faith perspective to help them see God at work in Jesus.

But obedience also requires faith. Preconceived, unbiblical notions about God make it even harder to act when he commands. How many blessings are we missing because of lack of faith or obedience? Obedience sometimes means living more simply than we would prefer, even if only for a season. Jesus knew the human propensity for attachment to material things; they can shackle us. He also knew the human struggle linked to rejection, so he warned it would come, and gave the Twelve and us freedom to walk away from persistent renunciation of Jesus.

Jesus the Carpenter?

Most translations of Mark 6:3 call Jesus a carpenter, but Matthew addressed him as the carpenter's son (13:55). Was Jesus a carpenter like his stepfather, Joseph, and why mention the occupation?

In Jewish culture, a son typically studied his father's occupation, and tradition holds Jesus learned carpentry, carrying on the family business after Joseph's death. To his patriarchal Jewish audience, Matthew's reference further legitimized Jesus as Joseph's legally adopted son. Such a statement was less relevant to Mark's Roman audience, so he focused on Jesus. Thus, both Gospel writers are correct.

The word *carpenter* comes from the word meaning "to create." While it included craftsmen of metals or stone, it primarily referred to woodworking handymen. Jesus probably had the skills and strength to make farming equipment, furniture, and structural materials for erecting small buildings.

Although not a despised occupation (such as shepherding), Jesus was an ordinary manual laborer. To the Nazarenes, Jesus should not have been expected to be extraordinary. He had a job that was not expected to produce an eloquent, well-versed public speaker or a miracle-worker. Even today people struggle to accept Jesus because he does not conform to their preconceptions.

We Are Family

Some believe that even after marriage Mary remained a virgin, interpreting Mark 6:3 to refer to Jesus' cousins or stepsiblings from Joseph and another woman. However, this claim lacks substantial Scriptural evidence.

The recorded siblings of Jesus include:

- James, who was probably next oldest, a leader in the Jerusalem church (Galatians 1:19; 2:1–9), likely authored the New Testament book of James, and probably died a martyr's death.

- Joseph and Simon, about whom we have no details.

- Judas, who likely authored the New Testament Book of Jude.

- Sisters, who were left unnamed as befit the culture. Mark and Matthew (13:56) nevertheless mentioned them.

Questions

1. Do you know people who cannot seem to let you grow up? How do you cope with them? What, if anything, can we learn from Jesus about dealing with such people? Are there ways in which we really are not spiritually mature? Have you acted like a villager of Nazareth in someone's life or spiritual journey? How can you change?

2. Luke 4:14–30 tells us Jesus read from Isaiah 61 when he spoke in the Nazarene synagogue. Review both passages and discuss why this so enraged the townspeople.

3. How does it affect you to consider Jesus might have lived under a cloud of suspicion and rumors about the legitimacy of his birth? Do you think that contributed to his inability to minister in Nazareth? Why or why not?

4. Jesus could do anything. Why did he choose to limit himself (Mark 6:5) because of human response? Do you think God limits himself in the lives of people today because of a lack of faith?

5. Share a personal experience of faith and miracles, of God providing when no one else could, or share a time when you believe a lack of faith prevented God's full expression of power.

6. How do we balance depending on God for necessities
    with taking the responsibility to provide for ourselves?
    How do they work in tandem? How do they work
    against one another?

7. Are we willing to totally depend on God's provision for
    the ministry assignments he gives us? Why do we often
    hesitate?

Notes

1. Name changed.

2. A risky proposition since he had been poorly received by the religious leaders at a previous synagogue (Mark 3:1–6); and as God Incarnate, he certainly knew the doubts of his listeners.

3. David E. Garland, *The NIV Application Commentary – Mark* (Grand Rapids, Michigan: Zondervan, 1996), 231.

4. Ibid.

5. Both practices were clearly important to Mark since he first introduced Jesus as a preacher in 1:14 and the first miracle he recorded was Jesus exorcising a demon (1:23–26).

6. Jesus and the early church continued this practice of paired ministry. See Mark 11:1; 14:3; Luke 10:1; Acts 13:1–4; 16:40.

lesson  6

Outward Piety vs. Inward Purity

MAIN IDEA

Jesus redefined the meaning and requirements of holiness.

QUESTION TO EXPLORE

To what man-made religious traditions are you clinging?

STUDY AIM

To evaluate my allegiance to man-made religious traditions and to embrace God's requirements for holiness

QUICK READ

Challenged by religious leaders, Jesus disagreed with them for using man-made laws to circumvent God-given instructions, and in so doing, exposed the utter sinfulness and depravity of the human heart.

Introduction

In Norman Jewison's classic musical *Fiddler on the Roof*, the lead character, Tevye, celebrates the traditions he has practiced and the expected roles he has held dear since his childhood, even singing the song "Tradition" with his fellow villagers. However, Tevye struggles when his world grows more complex. His daughters make personal choices that strain against the fundamental maxims of their society, and conflicting cultures encroach upon Tevye's traditional way of life.

Traditions have a way of either governing us or growing us, grounding us or grappling us. The Pharisees and scribes with whom Jesus dialogued were enslaved by tradition because they allowed its rules for holiness to drive their motives, instead of allowing their relationship with God to drive their behavior.

Jesus exposed this weakness and fundamentally redefined the meaning and requirements of holiness, contrasting man-made religious traditions with God's expectations. Unfortunately, many of us do not recognize the hypocrisy in our lives. We may fool ourselves into believing we act as God requires, but we fail to address root sins. As a result, we, like the Pharisees, have religion but not a healthy relationship with the God we claim to serve.

Mark 7:1–23

1 The Pharisees and some of the teachers of the law who had come from Jerusalem gathered around Jesus and **2** saw some of his disciples eating food with hands that were "unclean," that is, unwashed. **3** (The Pharisees and all the Jews do not eat unless they give their hands a ceremonial washing, holding to the tradition of the elders. **4** When they come from the marketplace they do not eat unless they wash. And they observe many other traditions, such as the washing of cups, pitchers and kettles.)

5 So the Pharisees and teachers of the law asked Jesus, "Why don't your disciples live according to the tradition of the elders instead of eating their food with 'unclean' hands?"

6 He replied, "Isaiah was right when he prophesied about you hypocrites; as it is written:

"'These people honor me with their lips,
     but their hearts are far from me.
7 They worship me in vain;
     their teachings are but rules taught by men.'

8 You have let go of the commands of God and are holding on to the traditions of men."

9 And he said to them: "You have a fine way of setting aside the commands of God in order to observe your own traditions! **10** For Moses said, 'Honor your father and your mother,' and, 'Anyone who curses his father or mother must be put to death.' **11** But you say that if a man says to his father or mother: 'Whatever help you might otherwise have received from me is Corban' (that is, a gift devoted to God), **12** then you no longer let him do anything for his father or mother.

13 Thus you nullify the word of God by your tradition that you have handed down. And you do many things like that."

14 Again Jesus called the crowd to him and said, "Listen to me, everyone, and understand this. **15** Nothing outside a man can make him 'unclean' by going into him. Rather, it is what comes out of a man that makes him 'unclean.' "

17After he had left the crowd and entered the house, his disciples asked him about this parable. **18** "Are you so dull?" he asked. "Don't you see that nothing that enters a man from the outside can make him 'unclean'? **19** For it doesn't go into his heart but into his stomach, and then out of his body." (In saying this, Jesus declared all foods "clean.")

20 He went on: "What comes out of a man is what makes him 'unclean.' **21** For from within, out of men's hearts, come evil thoughts, sexual immorality, theft, murder, adultery, **22** greed, malice, deceit, lewdness, envy, slander, arrogance and folly. **23** All these evils come from inside and make a man 'unclean.'"

Dirty Hands and Dirty Intentions (7:1–13)

In an undisclosed location in Galilee, Pharisees and scribes who traveled from Jerusalem approached Jesus to observe and converse with the rabbi who captured the attention of much of Israel (Mark 7:1). Perhaps some sincerely sought to discern if he were a teacher sent by God but most probably investigated him with jealous ambitions or hidden agendum. They found ammunition for their suspicions when they saw his disciples eat bread with unclean hands (7:2).[1]

Mark, for his predominantly Gentile readership, clarified this defilement: their hands were "unwashed" (Greek: *koinos*, meaning "common" or "ordinary;" i.e., not "set apart" or "holy"). Tradition, Mark explained in 7:3–4, prescribed Jews to cleanse themselves of any external sinful influence or exposure. This practice, grounded in Levitical instruction, required priests to wash before entering the tabernacle (Exodus 29:4; 30:17–21). All Jews were required to cleanse themselves following contact with anything associated with sin, sickness, or death (Leviticus 11:25; 13:6; 15:11, 22; 16:26–28).

Over the centuries, as religious leaders expounded upon these instructions (and others), the mass of rules about the law came to be known as the "tradition of the elders." These rules even specified cleansing from any non-Jewish place or association. Accidentally brushing a Gentile's shoulder necessitated ceremonial cleansing, which is why Mark mentioned the marketplace, a public forum where people of all races gathered. Furthermore, if Gentiles touched "cups, pitchers and kettles," (Mark 7:4) Jews were to wash them before using them to prepare food.

The purpose of these rules was to spread holiness throughout the culture, infusing full devotion into every aspect of life, even the mundane, so people might fully acknowledge God's sovereignty and have no questions about explicit obedience. Though well-intentioned, by the third century A.D., when all these verbal rules were finally written down as the *Mishnah*, the "tradition of the elders" had evolved to become as binding as God's written law, whereby obligation trumped character, in complete opposition to God's intent (Micah 6:6–8; Psalm 40:6–8; Hosea 6:4–7).

As the perceived keepers of the tradition, these leaders protested Jesus' disciples' disregard for the rules, asking him why they[2] ate with unclean hands (Mark 7:5). They were not worried, of course, about hygiene or sanitation. In a culture where reputation was everything, they were attempting to discredit Jesus publicly as an incompetent teacher.

However, Jesus was not influenced by public opinion. He taught and lived differently than the religious leaders. He ate with "tax collectors and sinners" (2:16), had a different perspective about fasting (2:18–20), and maintained the Sabbath had a fundamentally different purpose (2:23–28). They perceived him as a threat to the religious community because he seemed to be dismissing, or at least undermining, their understanding of a right relationship with God (not to mention their authority).

Rather than denying or confirming his disciples' guilt, Jesus addressed his accusers in Mark 7:6–8. While they sought to criticize external behaviors, Jesus drew attention to internal motives. Paraphrasing Isaiah 29:13, he said their hearts were neither pious nor surrendered to God (Deuteronomy 6:4–5), calling them "hypocrites," portraying them as actors who wore different masks during a play. Even though others might hear them honor God "with their lips," the religious leaders were playing roles ineffective to the audience that mattered—God. And although they labeled their practices as the tradition of the elders (Greek *presb-uteron* Mark 7:5) Jesus described their traditions as human (Greek *anthropon* 7:8), a small but significant difference.

Jesus then pointed out his accusers' passion for observing the oral teaching rather than God's written law (7:9). Although they were regarded as "experts in the law" (Luke 11:46, 52), Jesus highlighted their expertise in circumventing the law. He contrasted the "commands of God" with "your own traditions," implying the latter's origins were not God-ordained, an affront to these men who believed the Mosaic law and the tradition of the elders were equivalent. In so doing, however, Jesus subordinated acts that merely broke human tradition and validated the removal of traditions, no matter how beloved, that contradicted Scripture.

In Mark 7:10–13, Jesus specifically named one of these contradictory practices. Despite the fact God's law ("Moses said") dictated children must honor their parents (Exodus 20:12), oral teaching ("you say") circumvented the law by allowing a man to vow to God resources allocated for the care of aging parents, thus freeing him from the obligation. This practice, Mark explained, was as simple as calling something "Corban," meaning "given to God" (Mark 7:11), a concept appearing in the Books of Leviticus, Numbers, and Ezekiel.

Corban's original purpose was to reserve something for sacred use and prevent it from being profanely employed by another; it preserved the item/gift as if it were an offering. Thus, a man did not "necessarily promise [the item/gift] to the temple nor did he prevent its use for himself. What he did do was to exclude legally his parents from benefiting from it. [So, he] could continue to use and enjoy the property until death, at which time the remainder would presumably go to the temple."[3]

Unfortunately, if the man regretted his vow, he could not revoke it under the statute of Numbers 30:2. "When a man makes a vow to the LORD or takes an oath to obligate himself by a pledge, he must not break his word but must do everything he said." Thus, when Jesus said the leaders would not allow a man to do "anything" for his parents (7:12), he was not exaggerating. No provision was made for annulling such a vow in Jewish law until 220 A.D.

Jesus condemned the rules about Corban as nullifying (rendering powerless) God's word (7:13). He was disgusted by their willingness to use one biblical commandment to negate another; the law was not given for its own sake, but for the sake of humanity (Mark 2:27). And, as Jesus concluded in Mark 7:13, this was only one example of many where oral tradition offered legal loopholes for disobeying God's laws.

Dirty Hearts and Dirty Thoughts (7:14–23)

Turning his attention from the religious leaders to everyday people (7:14), Jesus expounded on actual defilement. He wanted the people to actually "understand" his message (Greek *suneido*; implying importance).

Jesus explained that purity was not the result of obedience to laws.[4] Most Jews at the time "thought of sin as a sort of germ, an infection caught by contact, [but] Jesus taught that sin was like a cancer growing within us."[5] This perspective was a radical concept. Jews believed external purity resulted in legal compliance, which would then earn righteousness before God. In contrast, Jesus taught that a right relationship with God–whereby a person has pure thoughts, words, and desires–would overflow into conduct congruent with God's desires as expressed in the laws he gave. Jesus said what comes out of people defiles them, not what goes into them (7:15).

In Mark 7:17, the scene shifted from the crowd to a private teaching session as Jesus and his disciples entered a house,[6] evidently a fairly standard practice following a time of public teaching.

Despite their ongoing relationship with Jesus, the disciples were equally uninformed on the subject of purity. Although some might read Jesus' tone in Mark 7:18 as sarcastic and condescending, the wording most likely represented a moment of discouragement for him as a teacher. After all the time his disciples had spent with him, they had not overcome the influence of Pharisaical indoctrination.

So, Jesus explained: God judges purity based on the heart (the source of thoughts, emotions, personality, motives and desires which determine actions or inactions; cf. 1 Samuel 16:7; Matt. 5:8). Nothing ingested can pollute a person's heart; food merely goes through the stomach and is excreted. (The parenthetical statement at the end of Mark 7:19 may have been commentary added by Mark or Peter in homage to Peter's vision recorded in Acts 10:9–16.)

In Mark 7:20, Jesus reiterated the message of 7:15b, listing specific indicators of unrighteousness (7:21–23), which begin as "evil thoughts" then emerge as overt sins (acts which directly affect others) or sinful attitudes or dispositions (moral defects or vices):

- sexual immorality (by the unmarried)
- theft
- murder
- adultery (sexual immorality by those who are married)
- greed (including lust)
- malice (deliberate wicked acts toward another)
- deceit (to lure or snare with bait; cunning or treachery)
- lewdness (unrestrained sexual instinct; open and shameless sensuality; vulgarity)
- envy (i.e., "evil eye;" jealously despising another)
- slander (hurtful speech about another)
- arrogance (prideful; braggadocious)
- folly (lack of sense, spiritual sensitivity, or moral judgment; not knowing God and not wishing to know him; foolishness).

Whether through overt sinful behaviors or less obvious sinful attitudes, we are all guilty of wickedness on Jesus' terms. We are defiled and in need of cleansing. Man-made solutions for purity will never accomplish God's purposes, nor restore fellowship with him. We need purification, and Christ offers the only path to it (Titus 2:11–14).

Implications and Actions

Following rules does not change the heart. Christ at work in us creates inside-out change that produces godly perspectives on holiness, people, and tradition. Jesus proved holiness does not need guardians to protect it with a fence of rules they enforce. "On the contrary, God's holiness transcends all boundaries. It does not suffer contamination but transforms everything it touches."[7]

Jesus' regular exposure to "uncleanness" (of which the religious leaders disapproved) brought transformation in the lives of the lepers he touched (Mark 1:41), corpses he raised (5:41), and hemorrhaging people he healed (5:27–29). Lives mattered more to him than laws.

Believers today can fall into the same trap as the Pharisees. When we create man-made expectations for spiritual growth or spiritual practices as markers of spiritual health or maturity, personal and communal peace may be disrupted. Traditions have their rightful place (see sidebar "Is Tradition Bad?"), but we must not hold them more tightly than the grace and freedom Christ offers (John 1:17; Galatians 5:1). Otherwise, we will not offer grace to those who differ from us, and we will become self-righteousness based on our definitions of holiness. Ultimately, the hearts of people mattered more to Jesus than religious tradition. They should also matter more to us.

Is Tradition Bad?

Tradition often gets a bad reputation, but Jesus did not reject tradition in and of itself. Commentator David E. Garland says, "Societies need traditions to function, [and] Jesus recognized we need wineskins—traditions—to hold the wine; otherwise, we will be standing in a puddle of juice. He warned only about wineskins that become old and brittle and no longer serve their intended purpose" (Mark 2:21–22). Traditions become:

- evil when they contradict God's ethical commands for relating to others
- dangerous when we are blind to how they undermine God's commands
- corrupt when we're more devoted to upholding them than obeying God's direct commands" [8]

The Root of the Problem

In the Sermon on the Mount, Jesus addressed root sins within a person's heart and mind. Anger with or condescension toward another, he said, are no less serious infractions than murder, and lust no less dangerous than adultery (Matt. 5:21–22, 27–29). To communicate how grievous these root sins are, he hyperbolically suggested removing body parts to prevent their repetition.

Romans 1:28–32 and 1 Timothy 3:1–5 also include lists of vices that expand upon what Jesus mentioned in the Book of Mark, but the uniqueness of Jesus' list in 7:21–22 is the parallelism found in the first six actions:

- sexual immorality–adultery

- theft–greed

- murder–malice

We cannot expect God to empty us of one vice and not have another take its place unless we allow the Holy Spirit to fill us (Ephesians 5:18b). He can root out the "evil thoughts" and substitute the characteristics of God's love we find in 1 Corinthians 13:4–8.

Ask God to make your heart rooted and grounded in love (Ephesians 3:17), instead of the patterns and behaviors of this world (1 John 2:15–17).

Questions

1. What "traditions of the elders" (not required by God) are treated as requirements in Christianity worldwide, Western Christianity, in your local body of believers, or in your faith journey?

2. What spiritual practices have you observed that neglect the well-being of people for the sake of keeping a rule?

3. What's the significance of Jesus calling laws *human* traditions instead of the traditions of the elders?

4. Since "nothing outside a man can make him 'unclean' by going into him" (Mark 7:15), some would suggest all movies, books, art, photography, and so forth are acceptable. What, if any, limitations should believers place on where we go, what we expose ourselves to, and what we choose to ingest mentally? Discuss your opinions based on your experience or observation. Does Scripture validate your statements?

5. Are there spiritual truths you struggle to believe and act upon just as the disciples did because of years of being taught or experiencing the wrong thing (Mark 7:17–19)? Name them and ask God to reveal to you the truth of his word in those areas so you can walk in truth (1 John 1:6; 2 John 1:4).

6. The list of sins in Mark 7:21–22 is not exhaustive, but it addresses the root of a multitude of sins. Carefully consider if you are guilty of any of these sins. The Holy Spirit does convict, but he is not the source of perpetual guilt. Confess your sin, repent, and receive the grace of forgiveness God so freely offers, then walk in the freedom and new life he provides.

Notes

1. Some speculate this bread was part of the leftover remaining from the feeding of the 5,000 (6:43) the afternoon before. In Luke 11:37–38, Jesus was condemned for the same infraction in the home of a Pharisee.

2. The leaders implicitly blame *all* the disciples, even though 7:2 states "*Some* of the disciples" (italics mine) had unwashed hands. The Greek word *tis*, translated "some" could mean as few as one.

3. James A. Brooks, "Mark," *The New American Commentary*, vol. 23 (Nashville: Broadman Press, 1991), 117.

4. Jesus never deprecated God's law, because he came to fulfill it, not abolish it (Matthew 5:17). He didn't necessarily differ with the Pharisees about the idea of clean hands, he just "rejected their approach to God's law." David E. Garland, *The NIV Application Commentary – Mark* (Grand Rapids, Michigan: Zondervan, 1996), 275.

5. D.A. Carson, Ed., "Mark," *New Bible Commentary*; Accordance/IVP-NB Commentary electronic ed., prepared by OakTree Software, Inc. (Downers Grove, IL: Intervarsity Press, 1994), 961.

6. Apparently, synagogues were too much a place of rejection, for Mark 6:2 was the last reference to Jesus teaching there. From this point forward, Jesus' teaching is primarily in homes and then in the Jerusalem temple.

7. Garland, 281.

8. Ibid., 277.

lesson 7

A Correct Confession and a Scathing Correction

MAIN IDEA

Peter correctly confessed Jesus as the Christ, but failed to recognize the nature of his mission.

QUESTION TO EXPLORE

What is the true nature of Jesus' mission?

STUDY AIM

To understand and embrace the challenging nature of discipleship

QUICK READ:

Having the correct answers does not guarantee a true understanding of Christ or discipleship. Jesus died but rose again, and he calls us to die to ourselves, following him exclusively.

Introduction

The Sea of Galilee region was familiar territory for Jesus and his disciples. Capernaum was Jesus' base of operations (Mark 2:1; Matthew 9:1), and probably James' and John's home. Bethsaida, the hometown of Andrew, Peter, and Philip, lay across the sea on the northern coast (John 1:44). From these familiar places, Jesus led his disciples about twenty-five miles north to Caesarea Philippi[1] (now known as Banias), an area of great beauty but deep spiritual darkness.

Caesarea Philippi had long been a religious center. In Old Testament times, Canaanites worshiped their god of good fortune, Baal-gad, there. Later, because of the area's lush vegetation and abundant water,[2] the Greeks dedicated a shrine to the god Pan (god of nature), calling the town Paneas. During the Roman Era, Herod the Great built a temple out of white marble, dedicating it to Emperor Augustus. After Herod had died, his son Philip ruled, rebuilding and renaming the city in honor of Tiberias Caesar and himself.

Mark 8:27–38

27 Jesus and his disciples went on to the villages around Caesarea Philippi. On the way he asked them, "Who do people say I am?"

28 They replied, "Some say John the Baptist; others say Elijah; and still others, one of the prophets."

29 "But what about you?" he asked. "Who do you say I am?" Peter answered, "You are the Christ."

30 Jesus warned them not to tell anyone about him.

31 He then began to teach them that the Son of Man must suffer many things and be rejected by the elders, chief priests and teachers of the law, and that he must be killed and after three days rise again. **32** He spoke plainly about this, and Peter took him aside and began to rebuke him.

33 But when Jesus turned and looked at his disciples, he rebuked Peter. "Get behind me, Satan!" he said. "You do not have in mind the things of God, but the things of men."

34 Then he called the crowd to him along with his disciples and said: "If anyone would come after me, he must deny himself and take up his cross and follow me. **35** For whoever wants to save his life will lose it, but whoever loses his life for me and for the gospel will save it.**36** What good is it for a man to gain the whole world, yet forfeit his soul? **37** Or what can a man give in exchange for his soul? **38** If anyone is ashamed of me and my words in this adulterous and sinful generation, the Son of Man will be ashamed of him when he comes in his Father's glory with the holy angels."

Mark 9:1

1And he said to them, "I tell you the truth, some who are standing here will not taste death before they see the kingdom of God come with power."

A Daring Declaration (8:27–30)

While walking to the villages surrounding Caesarea Philippi, which was so rich with religious connections, Jesus asked his disciples a profound question: "Who do people say I am?" (Mark 8:27). Perhaps they had been walking along, chatting about their families, the beautiful scenery, or recalling recent miracles, when, suddenly, Jesus at the lead, turned and inquired of them. Or maybe they had stopped to rest, and as they huddled around their teacher, he posed the query. Like many of Jesus' teaching methods, this approach was in direct opposition to Jewish custom in which disciples, not rabbis, asked questions.

The disciples' responses varied: John the Baptist; Elijah; or a prophet (8:28).[3] Jesus certainly knew these theories, so why did he ask the question? Mark 8:29 reveals Jesus was probing to see if they were more influenced by him or by the masses surrounding them. He was, in effect, guiding them to formulate and solidify their opinions and articulate them, not for his sake but theirs.

Was it was quiet for a moment as each man privately contemplated the question: *What should I say? Is there a right answer? What do I believe about his identity? How do express my thoughts without giving away too much of my vulnerability?* Then Peter announced, "You are the Messiah."[4] It was a daring declaration. The Messiah was the one for whom Jews had waited for centuries (see sidebar "You Are the Messiah"). In the region of Caesarea Philippi, where pagans professed faith in man-made idols, Peter boldly professed faith in his rabbi as the fulfillment of Israel's prophetic hopes and dreams. While he likely spoke on behalf of the other disciples, we do not know with certainty that this was the case.

Though Peter's confession was correct, it was inadequate. None of the disciples had a complete view of Jesus' messianic calling: the deep implications, suffering, and cost. However, until he died and rose again, it was not completely necessary for others to recognize him as Messiah, so Jesus commanded them to remain silent about his identity (8:30). Silence also prevented the spread of misinformation. To help them unlearn everything believed about the Messiah's role,[5] Jesus told them what would happen to him, and they did not like what they heard.

A Difficult Dialogue (8:31–33)

Suffering and rejection are rarely part of any plan. Thus, when Jesus began to teach his disciples that he "must suffer many things and be rejected . . ." (new information to their ears) Peter recoiled in resistance and disapproval. Rejection by the elders, chief priests, and teachers of the law was catastrophic; they were the movers and shakers, the ones Jesus needed on his side to overthrow the Romans. They had influence, money, and connections.

When Jesus said he would be killed, the disciples were shocked; they did not want to lose their friend and rabbi (8:31). After all, how could one who had silenced storms, cast out demons, healed infirmities, fed thousands, and forgiven sins become a murder victim? Nor did Jesus offer room for an alternate plan. Instead, he emphasized the Son of Man, must ("binding," or "according to divine will"), experience these things. But this scenario did not fit the disciples' cosmology for a glorious and powerful leader. Jesus told them these things "plainly" (8:32), and concealed nothing. It was important that they understood what it meant for him to be the Messiah, and to later verify everything that happened as the fulfillment of God's plan (also cf. Isaiah 52:13–53:12).

Peter understood the gravity of what Jesus described, and was disgruntled. He ignored Jesus' promise of resurrection and called Jesus aside to admonish him (Mark 8:32.) The modern definition of the word *rebuke* is "a stern reprimand." However, the Greek word for rebuke is *nouthesia*, which means "to call attention to" as a warning or encouragement to "settle down," so the admonishment might have been less caustic than we imagine. Regardless of how politely Peter tried to discourage Jesus from talking about things to come, Jesus looked at him and the other disciples, and responded, "Get behind me, Satan!" (8:33; lit. *go back away, Satan*).

It is tempting to think Jesus was excessively harsh or unkind. However, Jesus knew Peter's struggle was not against flesh and blood, but against the spiritual forces of evil (Ephesians 6:12). He addressed the root problem: Satan was using Peter to tempt Jesus just as he had in the wilderness (Matthew 4:1–11; Mark 1:12–13). Once again, Satan wanted to suggest that disobedience to God's plan would not effectively change the outcome of God's will; Jesus could find glorification through some other method.

But God's ways and thoughts are different and unexpected (cf. Isaiah 55:8–9; 1 Corinthians 1:23, 25), thus, Peter and the disciples, focused on the physical and temporal, were not seeing the eternal picture. Peter, like many of us, wanted Jesus to do things according to his design, but that is not a disciple's role. A disciple is a student, a follower. Getting Jesus' title correct is merely the first step. In the next verses, Jesus explicitly stated his demands for all disciples to a gathering crowd.

A Demanding Discourse (8:34–9:1)

Where did the crowd come from in this distant region? What was Jesus doing in the villages surrounding Caesarea Philippi that drew idol-worshipping people? We do not know; however, one thing is certain—true followers of Jesus will better understand the necessity of Jesus' sufferings, not by merely observing them but by participating in them (cf. Philippians 3:10; 2 Corinthians 4:8–11).

Jesus outlined three demands for each of his disciples (8:34):

1. *Deny yourself*
Jesus did not ask his disciples to deny a *thing*. That is self-discipline or asceticism. Jesus asked something far greater; he expected the Twelve (and us)

to renounce self as the object of life's affection by fundamentally reorienting our egocentricity to God-centricity. He called his disciples, just as he calls us, to reject following natural desires and personal rights (for good or evil) in favor of God's desires; loving him so much that serving him and others take priority, no matter the cost. It is willingly saying with confidence, "not my will, but yours" (Luke 22:42), despite a culture that advocates, "advance yourself, even if you wound others."

2. *Take up your cross*

The cross was an object of rejection, scorn, and embarrassment in Roman times. Crucifixion was a method of execution reserved for heinous criminals and slaves because it exacted extreme torture and cruelty. No one survived a crucifixion.

Jesus called his disciples to martyrdom. He calls us to the same. Martyrdom is defined, not as enduring an "irritation or even a major burden, [but rather a] willingness to give up everything dear in life and even life itself"[6] for the sake of Jesus and others. It is a sobering, even macabre thought that should be repugnant to our ears if we take it with the gravity Jesus intended. His statement to his disciples would have conjured a visual image of a condemned person carrying a cross through public venues to the execution site. The path to that place (just as it was for

Jesus) was marked with torturous beatings, mocking insults, and exhausting steps. For us, Jesus' edict means our journey will not be easy because the cross represents suffering and oppression inflicted upon us by humanity, yet it is something for which we should volunteer in a spirit of self-sacrifice.

3. Follow me (lit. follow after me)
When Jesus called the Twelve to follow him (Matt. 1; Mark 4), they responded immediately, according to his specifications. When the men described in Matthew 8:18–22 and Luke 9:57–62 requested to follow Jesus, they wanted to set their own parameters. With such preconditions, Jesus declared them unfit for service in his kingdom (Luke 9:62). Disciples must go when Jesus calls and emulate him in word and deed.

As the rationale for accepting his demands, Jesus appealed to the innate human desire for security by offering a surprising paradox: in losing our lives, we are saved (Mark 8:35). Those who deny Christ to survive will actually bring about their eternal death. However, giving up our lives for Christ's sake results in life from God, the giver of life eternal (John 4:14), life abundant (John 10:10), and every good and perfect gift (James 1:17).[7]

Jesus' rhetorical question posed in Mark 8:36 assumes nothing is valuable enough to substitute for a person's eternal soul. How many people daily pursue money, pleasures, and possessions, ultimately gaining nothing but absolute loss? Nor is there any way someone can regain eternal life with Christ if he or she denies him (8:37). It is a solemn warning because the judgment is coming, when the truth will expose our choices. Those who reject association with Christ (8:38) choose poorly. He will deny them entrance into heaven when he returns, glorious and victorious.

Finally, Jesus issued a confident promise: all will someday see the power of God's kingdom, but some will see it realized in their lifetime (9:1). Jesus' words here are unwavering: he began with "truly I tell you" (lit. *amen,* meaning "surely," "so be it") a phrase indicating the trustworthiness of what follows. Then he used the strongest negative possible to emphasize death would not come upon some of those standing with him.

We can identify at least six experiences where God's power was on fantastic display following this pronouncement: (1) the Transfiguration; (2) his continued performance of miracles; (3) his resurrection and appearances; (4) his ascension into heaven; (5) Pentecost; and (6) signs and wonders performed by the early church. Those who hold fast to their confession will find Christ is faithful (Hebrews 3:6), and the confident assurance that nothing done for the sake of the gospel is in vain.

Implications and Actions

Six days after the conversations in this passage, Jesus led Peter, James, and John up a high mountain (probably farther north onto Mt. Hermon), where he was transfigured (Mark 9:2–4). Though they were Jesus' closest friends, what he revealed about himself to them was far beyond their expectations. Despite the miracles they saw Jesus perform and the declaration of Jesus as Messiah, they saw his divinity firsthand in a brilliant display. In this unfamiliar place, where spiritual darkness was so prevalent, Jesus demonstrated a small portion of his glory (cf. Luke 2:32; Revelation 21:23), and it humbled Peter, James, and John (Matt. 17:6).

Many believers want to cling to this brilliant, final image of Jesus and bypass the pain and suffering of the Messiah. Likewise, we want our journey to be without cost or humility. Although we might not confront Jesus as Peter did, we nevertheless do not want following Christ to be difficult, unpopular, uncomfortable, or inconvenient. We certainly do not want to deny ourselves. For each of us, taking up our cross means sacrificing personal desires, preferences, plans, and sometimes dreams in obedience to Christ.

In light of his suffering, how do you need to redefine discipleship as you follow Jesus today?

You Are the Messiah

The word *Messiah* was originally an adjective meaning "anointed," referring to something or someone chosen, consecrated, and given power by God to accomplish an assigned task. Later, it evolved into a title ("the anointed one"), meaning a specific and ideal individual who would come in God's power and overthrow all foreign rule, reestablishing Israel with glory as an independent nation. Knowing these expectations were man-made and not his actual purpose, Jesus allowed others to refer to him as Messiah, but he rarely spoke of himself with the title. By the time Paul wrote his letters, he had substituted the Greek word *Christos* (Christ), which also means "Anointed One."

Predicted in the Old Testament (e.g., Daniel 7:13–14; Jeremiah 33:14–18; Zechariah 6:12–13), the Messiah would establish a kingdom in which peace, purpose, and prosperity existed for all. He would be a godly spiritual leader serving as priest and prophet, a benevolent ruler of God's people, and a mighty conqueror of Israel's enemies. Though Jesus is all these things, his kingdom is not of this world (John 18:36).

Son of Man

The title *Son of Man,* an Aramaic idiom, was Jesus' favorite personal reference. In the passage for this lesson, it is significant because it follows Peter's confession of him as Messiah. Jesus was not correcting Peter. Instead, he was revealing how the two titles (both prophesied in the Old Testament) work in tandem.

Daniel's vision of the Son of Man (7:13–14) illuminates the Messiah's eternal role (Revelation 11:15; 12:10). He:

110

- comes on the clouds (cf. Matt. 26:64; Rev. 1:7)
- has all authority (cf. Matt. 18:18), power, and glory (cf. Matt. 24:30; Rev. 5:12–13)
- has the worship of all nations (cf. Rev. 7:9–12)
- is everlasting (cf. Hebrews 1:8)

Questions

1. If Jesus asked you the questions he asked his disciples (Mark 8:27, 29), how would you respond? What do lost people you know say about him? Obviously, the responses of "John the Baptist, Elijah, or one of the prophets" (8:28) were wrong, but what made them so inadequate?

2. Would you have been obedient to Jesus' warning not to tell anyone his identity as Messiah? Would you have been more or less likely to obey after Jesus described the suffering and death he would endure? Why or why not?

3. If you had been one of the Twelve, would you have been the spokesperson like Peter, disapproving of Jesus' talk, or would you have kept quiet? Though we may be surprised by his impudence, have there been times when you wanted God to operate with a different plan? How would you have responded when Jesus rebuked this temptation so forcefully?

4. Describe a recent temptation to do something in disobedience to God's design because of someone else's expectations. Many modern-day church leaders face this struggle as parishioners place expectations on them. Prayerfully consider if you are a source of this temptation in someone's life.

5. It is tempting to seek security physically, emotionally, and financially rather than risk full surrender to Christ. Is there a difference between being secure and feeling secure? Review Jesus' parable in Luke 12:16–21 and compare/contrast it to his teaching in Mark 8:34–37 and Luke 12:22–34, and to Solomon's words in Ecclesiastes 2:17–23; 3:1–11; and 5:10–20.

6. Jesus took three of his disciples to an unfamiliar place to examine their faith and challenge them toward difficult obedience; then he took them farther up the mountain to reveal more about his divine nature and character in a way that humbled and awed them. Has God ever led you (literally or figuratively) through a similar experience? Where was it/how did it happen and what were the results? What did you learn about him? What did you learn about yourself?

Notes

1. In contrast to Caesarea Maritima on the Mediterranean Sea. On the border between the Holy Land and Gentile territory, this area was ruled by Herold Philip, not Herod Antipas, so neither the latter nor the religious leaders would likely molest them.

2. It was situated on the southern base of the Mt. Hermon mountain range and overlooks the northern end of the Jordan River Valley.

3. Herod Anitpas feared he was John, whom he thought he'd effectively beheaded (Mark 6:16). Though Jews knew Elijah's appearance meant the end times had come (Malachi 4:5), they didn't recognize John the Baptist as the precursor to the Messiah (Luke 1:17; Matthew 17:12; Mark 9:13). "One of the prophets" was a lower view of Jesus, neglecting his uniqueness from other prophets, past or present. Nevertheless, public opinion was actually better than Nazarean thought (that he was an average guy or mentally unstable) or that of the religious leaders, who thought Satan controlled him.

4. Mark began his narrative describing Jesus as the Messiah (Mark 1:1), but 8:29 is the first time he's mentioned the word since then. Peter's confession "occurs in the very center of [Mark's] Gospel, [hinging] the first half . . . where Jesus' power is so prominent, and the second half, where his weakness becomes prominent." David E. Garland, *The NIV Application Commentary – Mark* (Grand Rapids, Michigan: Zondervan, 1996), 323.

5. "They will learn the lesson with difficulty. Nothing happens as they expect or wish. Everyone has trouble learning that victory comes through giving one's life, not by taking others' lives." Garland, 331.

6. James A. Brooks, "Mark," *The New American Commentary*, vol. 23 (Nashville: Broadman Press, 1991), 137.

7. An encouraging word for Mark's Roman church and any believer who might consider denying Christ in the face of persecution.

lesson  8

Overcoming Unbelief

MAIN IDEA

Placing faith in an all-powerful God leads to limitless possibilities.

QUESTION TO EXPLORE

Where do you need Jesus to help you overcome your unbelief?

STUDY AIM

To place my full trust in Jesus as I face seemingly impossible obstacles

QUICK READ

All of us struggle with maintaining confidence and steadfast faith when faced with a crisis. However, entrusting our lives and difficulties into God's mighty hands unleashes myriads of possibilities and resources.

Introduction

Has someone you love ever received a diagnosis of a medical condition that was untreatable? Did the pronouncement propel you into discouragement and despair? Or, did the situation challenge you to exercise your faith and boldly approach God on behalf of your loved one? Often our faith in God confidently strides to the forefront ready to take on the world when something is beyond the remedies of human intervention. Sometimes, however, doubts weigh us down, and we need God to lift up our waning faith.

What do you do when a loved one's life is in jeopardy, and God is the only hope? Most of us do what the father in this lesson's Bible passage did. We come to God, urgently seeking his intervention and help. We desperately implore God to rescue our loved one and honor our sometimes less than steadfast faith. Earlier in Mark 9, Peter, James, and John experienced a mountaintop moment with God. As Jesus transfigured before them, they saw a dazzling display of the deity and glory of Jesus (9:1–8). However, when they came down the mountain, they entered a valley of spiritual darkness where they encountered the lows of human opposition (9:14), and the destructive nature of evil as revealed in a demon-possessed boy.[1]

Mark 9:14–29

14 When they came *back* to the disciples, they saw a large crowd around them, and some scribes arguing with them. **15** Immediately, when the entire crowd saw Him, they were amazed and *began* running up to greet Him. **16** And He asked them, "What are you discussing with them?" **17** And one of the crowd answered Him, "Teacher, I brought You my son, possessed with a spirit which makes him mute; **18** and whenever it seizes him, it slams him to the ground and he foams at the *mouth*, and grinds his teeth and stiffens out. I told Your disciples to cast it out, and they could not do it." **19** And He answered them and said, "O unbelieving generation, how long shall I be with you? How long shall I put up with you? Bring him to Me!" **20** They brought the boy to Him. When he saw Him, immediately the spirit threw him into a convulsion, and falling to the ground, he began rolling around and foaming at the *mouth*. **21** And He asked his father, "How long has this been happening to him?" And he said, "From childhood. **22** It has often thrown him both into the fire and into the water to destroy him. But if You can do anything, take pity on us and help us!" **23** And Jesus said to him, "'If You can?' All things are possible to him who believes." **24** Immediately the boy's father cried out and said, "I do believe; help my unbelief." **25** When Jesus saw that a crowd was rapidly gathering, He rebuked the unclean spirit, saying to it, "You deaf and mute spirit, I command you, come out of him and do not enter him again." **26** After crying out and throwing him into terrible convulsions, it came out; and the boy became so much like a corpse that most of them said, "He is dead!" **27** But Jesus took him by the hand and raised him; and he got up. **28** When He came into the house, His disciples began questioning Him privately, "Why could we not drive it out?" **29** And He said to them, "This kind cannot come out by anything but prayer."

Unbelief and Misplaced Faith Are Counterproductive (9:14–19)

All of us have times when our faith seems to be humming on all cylinders, and every prayer is miraculously answered, even before the words leave our mouths. But we also have times when it seems like the engine of our faith has stalled, rendering us powerless. While our goal is to embrace consistent, constant, high-capacity faith, we do not always attain that goal. Neither did Jesus' disciples.

While Peter, James, and John were on the mountain of transfiguration with Jesus, the other nine disciples remained in the valley. All the disciples had experienced exhilaration when Jesus had empowered them and sent them to preach repentance, cast out demons, and heal people in his name. So when a man came seeking Jesus, who was still on the mountain, the disciples attempted to cast an evil spirit out of his son. They assumed the demon would depart as many had done earlier in their ministry (Mark 6:7–13).

As Jesus, Peter, James, and John came down the mountain and approached the others, they saw a large crowd surrounding the disciples, and heard some scribes arguing with them (9:14). The topic of the argument centered on the unsuccessful removal of an evil spirit from the boy. The scribes made political hay out of the situation, seeking to discredit Jesus and his disciples in the eyes of the people.

Surely it was a low moment for the disciples. By faith, they had tried to remove the demon and failed. They doubted their ability to serve God.

The faith of the boy's father was also at low tide. His son was demon-possessed, and the evil spirit did many destructive things to the boy (9:18). The father came to Jesus as his only hope for his son's freedom. He had faith to believe it could happen; he believed what he had heard about Jesus' power. He had the faith to make the journey and faith to make the request.

But when the boy's father arrived, Jesus was not there. The father asked the disciples to cast out the demon, but they failed. The man was trying to stay afloat in a sea of doubts, but waves of unbelief besieged him. Had he placed his faith in the disciples instead of in Jesus? Was God not strong enough to override the destructive forces in the life of his son?

We do not know why the disciples could not dispel the demon. Perhaps their faith was in their past successes instead of being rooted in the activity of God in the present moment. Perhaps they had not prepared themselves spiritually, for Jesus later said, "This kind cannot come out by anything but prayer" (9:29). Regardless of the reasons, the failure to remove the demon had wounded and unsettled their confidence. The failure was still bothering them when they later asked Jesus to tell them why they could not cast out the demon (9:28).

Faith Must Be Jesus-Centered (9:19–23)

When Jesus entered the scene, several things happened. Immediately the crowd that had gathered around the disciples saw Jesus and ran to meet him. The real power of faith is found in the person of Jesus, not in the personalities of his followers. Jesus asked what they were debating, and the father of the demon-possessed boy told Jesus how the disciples had been unable to free his son from the demon. He described the symptoms that occurred whenever his son was under the evil spirit's influence.

It is interesting to note that whenever Jesus steps into a situation, he becomes the center and focus of the event. Before Jesus arrived, the crowd was focused on all kinds of things. But once Jesus appeared, he became the central figure of the story. The crowd rushed to meet him, and the father brought his need directly to Jesus.

Jesus admonished those present about unbelief (Mark 9:19). The opportunity had arrived for them to enter the kingdom of God as they connected with God through Jesus. To achieve this connection, faith and trust in Jesus was mandatory. After all, Jesus was not going to be present physically with them much longer.

The disciples needed to learn to draw upon the power of God. They had to learn to discern what the Father was doing and join God in his work. They needed to rely on the power of God to overcome any unbelief or obstacles that stood in the way of accomplishing God's will.

Jesus had the solution to the problem. Indeed, Jesus was that solution. "Bring him to me," he said (9:19). Jesus has the power to evoke change, not his disciples. Jesus has power over the demonic, not us. Jesus can heal, not us. Our job is to bring people into contact with Jesus because he can do more than we dream possible.

Jesus interviewed the father, much like a modern doctor would. This interaction demonstrated the compassion and humanity of Jesus. Though fully God in human form, Jesus was also fully human. He did not neglect the psychological and emotional needs of the people to whom he ministered, nor their dignity. We should not ignore these needs as well.

They brought the boy to Jesus, and as soon as he entered Jesus' presence, the spirit became violent, trying to damage the boy. The descriptions found in verses 20–22, reveal the destructive nature of evil. Evil tries to immobilize and control people, silence and humiliate them and sometimes kill them.

The time had arrived for faith to become action. In Mark 9:22 the father put his faith into action when he said: "But if you can do anything, take pity on us and help us!" The man's faith was not bold enough to demand everything. Whereas he had told the disciples to cast the demon out (9:18), he only asked Jesus for pity. Previously he expected total restoration of his son's health and freedom, but now he was willing to settle for any help Jesus could provide.

In Mark 9:22–24, note the beautiful relational development between the boy's father and Jesus. The father asked, "if you can do anything . . ." (9:22). Jesus' response ("If you can!") was akin to Jesus asking, "If I can?" Jesus' desire or ability to cast out the demon was not in question. Jesus responded, "All things are possible to him who believes." In verse 23, the word "believes" functions as a present participle, which denotes ongoing action—"is believing, trusting." Thus the phrase "who believes" is not translated as "who is believing a dogma or truth" but rather one "who is believing and trusting God." The openness between Jesus and this man was wonderful. Jesus said: "All things are possible to him who is believing or trusting." The father's response communicated, "I do believe, Lord, help me overcome my moments of unbelief."

Active Faith Changes Lives (9:25–29)

Immediately upon hearing the father confess that he believed Jesus could heal his son, Jesus took action. He rebuked the evil spirit and commanded him to leave the boy's body and to never return (9:25). The spirit cried out (through a person who had been mute), threw him into some final convulsions, and departed.

After the departure of the evil spirit, the boy was lifeless, most of those watching thought he was dead. "But Jesus took him by the hand and raised him; and he got up" (9:27).

This was a new beginning. The boy's struggle with this demon was over. Jesus had defeated evil and then raised up the boy to a new life. The Greek words used here and translated "raised him up" are the same words used later to describe Jesus' resurrection from the dead (Mark 14:28; Acts 4:10; 5:30). The entire event was another message to the disciples that Jesus would die and rise from the dead (Mark 9:9–10). His death would not be the end of hope. Instead, it was a fresh beginning that would give new life to all who believe. In Jesus, the old life ends, and new life begins.

Implications and Actions

Active faith requires trusting God. Our belief and trust must be placed in Jesus (God) alone. All things are possible for those who actively believe God will faithfully fulfill his promises.

After casting out the demon, Jesus and the disciples withdrew into a house (9:28–29). The disciples were in turmoil as to why they could not cast out the demon. Jesus' answer? "This kind cannot come out by anything but prayer."

Prayer is an interactive connection and communion with Jesus. We are never the power source through which miraculous things occur. Only Jesus has this power. He has the name above all names and all power in heaven and earth. As we pray and live empowered by him, he will do amazing things through us as well.

Our responsibility is to believe steadfastly in the presence and power of Jesus, to bring people to him (9:19), and to encourage people to entrust themselves to Jesus. As people place their trust in him, Jesus changes their lives. The old life is gone, and new life begins. All things are possible for those who believe in Jesus (9:23).

Epilepsy or Demon Possession?

The symptoms described by the boy's father are similar to those of epilepsy; therefore, some may be tempted to say this was a medical condition rather than demonic possession. However, several things in the text support a demonic-spirit-induced malady:

- The father stated the boy was possessed by a spirit (Mark 9:17).

- Mark used verbs in verse 18 that denote the boy's body was hurled to the ground with force and thrown into waters and fire.

- Jesus recognized the demonic spirit, spoke to it as a being (i.e., you, rather than an "it"), called it an unclean, mute and dumb spirit, and ordered the spirit to come out of the boy and never return (9:25). These factors confirm an evil spirit caused this boy's symptoms and not a physiological disorder.

What is Effective Faith?

- It is presently active. "Faith is . . ." (Hebrews 11:1).
- It believes and trusts God to be who he says he is (Heb. 11:6).
- It believes God rewards faith placed in him (Heb. 11:6).
- It trusts Jesus to take action (Mark 9:23–24).
- It opens up endless possibilities because it connects us to a great God through whom all things are possible.

Questions

1. Why does it often seem that we are confronted with problems immediately after experiencing a spiritual "mountaintop" experience?

2. Where do you struggle with unbelief? Have you confessed this to God and asked for help?

3. What limitless possibility could you pursue with a renewed faith in God?

4. What is the condition of your prayer life? How could it become more powerful?

5. When you think of the word *faith*, what image comes to your mind?

Notes

1. Unless otherwise indicated, all Scripture quotations in lessons 8–10 are from the New American Standard Bible (1995 edition).

lesson  9

Greatness Equals Sacrifice

MAIN IDEA

Jesus corrected the misconception of his followers by clearly stating the purpose of his passion.

QUESTION TO EXPLORE

How do you define greatness?

STUDY AIM

To evaluate my definition of greatness and to choose to follow Jesus' example

QUICK READ

Jesus' response to James' and John's request for prominent positions in his kingdom redefined the meaning of greatness.

Introduction

How do you define greatness? What are the characteristics you esteem in others? Your list may include observable things: incredible intelligence, attractive, popular with others, witty, a global thinker, able to get things done, etc. Your list may also include tangible benchmarks: financially successful, well-connected, famous, successful track record, opulent homes and possessions.

Or, perhaps you would list character traits indicative of a great person. If so, your list might include: charismatic personality, truthful, trustworthy, faithful, committed, persevering, kind, generous, helpful, sensitive to others, polite, respectful.

Greatness is somewhat difficult to define because it can manifest itself in one's attitudes, values, character traits, actions, behavior, or in results produced in the workplace. In this lesson, we will explore what Jesus said should characterize greatness in our lives as his followers.

Mark 10:32–45

32 They were on the road going up to Jerusalem, and Jesus was walking on ahead of them; and they were amazed, and those who followed were fearful. And again He took the twelve aside and began to tell them what was going to happen to Him, **33** saying, "Behold, we are going up to Jerusalem, and the Son of Man will be delivered to the chief priests and the scribes; and they will condemn Him to death and will hand Him over to the Gentiles. **34** They will mock Him and spit on Him, and scourge Him and kill Him, and three days later He will rise again."

35 James and John, the two sons of Zebedee, came up to Jesus, saying, "Teacher, we want You to do for us whatever we ask of You."**36** And He said to them, "What do you want Me to do for you?" **37** They said to Him, "Grant that we may sit, one on Your right and one on Your left, in Your glory." **38** But Jesus said to them, "You do not know what you are asking. Are you able to drink the cup that I drink, or to be baptized with the baptism with which I am baptized?" **39** They said to Him, "We are able." And Jesus said to them, "The cup that I drink you shall drink; and you shall be baptized with the baptism with which I am baptized. **40** But to sit on My right or on My left, this is not Mine to give; but it is for those for whom it has been prepared."

41 Hearing this, the ten began to feel indignant with James and John.**42** Calling them to Himself, Jesus said to them, "You know that those who are recognized as rulers of the Gentiles lord it over them; and their great men exercise authority over them. **43** But it is not this way among you, but whoever wishes to become great among you shall be your servant; **44** and whoever wishes to be first among you shall be slave of all. **45** For even the Son of Man did not come to be served, but to serve, and to give His life a ransom for many."

The Greatness of Courage During Life's Journey (10:32–34)

The events described in the Scripture passage for this lesson occurred during the time of Passover. Jesus was on his way to Jerusalem. He was entering the final days of his life; his impending betrayal and crucifixion were unavoidable.

Great people are often courageous, or perhaps courageous people become great. Remarkable courage is sometimes demanded of people to travel the road ahead and face the challenges of life. Jesus was on a collision course with a brutal death. He knew this, but was energized by his mission and walked ahead of the disciples on the arduous, twenty-mile, uphill trek to Jerusalem. The disciples, who lagged behind, watched with amazement and fear as Jesus displayed composure and courage. Rather than shrink away, Jesus picked up the pace as he moved toward those who would kill him (Mark 10:32–34).

Courageous people lead the way through example, even when they know they will encounter opposition and perhaps cruelty. Jesus was leading the way up the hill, approaching the challenges ahead. Great people move forward to accomplish what is necessary and are often several steps ahead of others.

We see the greatness of courage in the clarity with which Jesus described what awaited him in Jerusalem (10:33–34). Previously he had taught the disciples that he was going to be rejected, killed, and would rise on the third day (8:31;

9:31). But within days of his death, he gave more details of this part of his journey. He would be betrayed, given over to the chief priests and Jewish leaders, condemned to death, turned over to the Romans, mocked, spit on, whipped, and killed. And three days later he would rise from the dead (10:33–34). Few people would quicken their pace with this agenda awaiting them.

Are you navigating an uphill battle in your life? Does brutal conflict or an unpleasant event loom large on the road ahead? Are you dragging your feet, or pressing on to accomplish the difficult, but necessary challenge that lies ahead?

The Greatness of Obedience (10:35–40)

During the journey, James and John approached Jesus. They were the sons of Zebedee (and some think that their mother was Salome, the sister of Mary, Jesus' mother). James and John asked Jesus to give them whatever they asked of him, to say, "Yes, it's yours" before they made their request (10:35).

Jesus asked what they desired him to do for them. They asked for positions of power, influence, and prestige, second only to Jesus (10:37). They wanted to rule with him. As children, they were taught that when the Messiah came, he would establish a physical kingdom, lead military conquests, and restore Israel to the glory days of David and Solomon.

Jesus popped their egotistic balloons: "You do not know what you are asking" (10:38). James and John imagined adulation, ruling like princes, and controlling others. Jesus was facing betrayal, rejection, cursing, humiliation, whips, and dying on a cross, naked before the world.

Jesus used the metaphors "cup" and "baptism" to depict what he was to face—and to confront James and John with what they would need to do to experience glory. Jesus asked them if they could drink the cup he was to drink and go through the waters of death that he would go through (10:38). Then, Jesus answered the questions he had asked. "The cup that I drink you shall drink; and you shall be baptized with the baptism with which I am baptized" (10:39). Baptism here probably refers not to the religious sacrament, but rather to the metaphorical meaning of baptism. Baptism signifies the death and burial of self-will through Christ and resurrection by the power of God to a new kind of life with Christ. James and John would both suffer and go through hardships because of their commitment to Jesus.

The cup Jesus was to drink was his obedient, sacrificial death on our behalf (2 Corinthians 5:21). Willingness to sacrifice self so that others can come to know God reveals true greatness. In the Garden of Gethsemane, Jesus prayed, asking God that if there were any other way to accomplish the world's salvation, let the cup of suffering, humiliation, pain, and death pass from him. However, there was an addendum to Jesus' prayer: ". . . not what I will, but what you will "(Mark 14:36). We exhibit greatness and sacrificial love for God when we are willing to lay down our lives, if necessary, for others to come to know him (John 15:13).

Greatness of Service (10:41–45)

Jesus corrected James and John in two ways for seeking positions of prestige and power. First, Jesus explained that God the Father is the decision maker. Second, greatness in God's kingdom is exemplified through acts of humble service, not self-promotion and power-grabbing.

The other disciples responded with indignation to the request of James and John (10:41). Was it righteous indignation because they did not believe James and John were worthy of such positions? Or, were they angry because the duo had beaten them to the punch?

Today, we often use secular standards to identify greatness, assuming that God values larger churches as greater than smaller ones, and that leaders of large ministries will certainly have the biggest rewards in heaven. But Jesus taught that we are not to use the number of people led, nor power-positions held, as measurements of greatness (10:42).

Power does not dictate spiritual greatness. Greatness in God's kingdom is about relinquishing power and serving others. It is not about how many people serve you; it is about how many people you serve (10:43–44).

The disciples were defining greatness as power, prestige, and position—ruling over others. But for Jesus, greatness was shown in surrendering power, laying aside prestige, and taking on the role of a servant (Philippians 2:5–8). Greatness was giving his life as a ransom for many (Mark 10:45). The word *ransom* depicts that which is paid or given in exchange

133

for freeing a captive. Sin held us captive, as did Satan. Jesus paid the price of his life to free us and restore our relationship with God.

For more than eleven years, I served in a large international organization comprised of Christians, many of whom were ordained ministers. One would think that working for such an organization would be a foretaste of heaven. In reality, just as in any large corporation, many employees used any means possible to attain higher positions in the organization. The organization included Christian leaders who practiced authoritarian leadership and perceived "boss" positions as any secular person would.

However, others in the organization modeled Christ-like leadership. One of my favorite memories involves a vice president of the organization who was a guest in my home. After a late-night conversation, I left the dinner dishes in the sink. The next morning, I walked into the kitchen and witnessed the organization's vice president washing those dishes. This encounter with character and humility made a deep and lasting impression upon me. Some leaders lead by demanding that others serve them. Others lead by demonstrating humble service to those who, based on an organizational chart, should be serving them.

Implications and Actions

Greatness comes in many forms and expresses itself in many ways. It is hard to define but easy to recognize. Whether we wish to be a great person, parent, Christian, or employee, the greatness formula includes a few basic things.

Great people honor God. They follow the example of Jesus in their values, priorities, and the way they treat other people. They live their lives to carry out God's will, not personal agendas. Great people treat those around them as more valuable than themselves. Greatness is manifested in our lives when these attitudes, values, and characteristics become a consistent part of our daily character and behavior.

How to Practice Greatness

- Serve others (Mark 10:43)
- Attend to the practical needs of those you serve (10:44)
- Live a consistent example of humility and sacrificial service (10:45)
- Value others more than yourself (10:45)
- Give up your desires so others can know and serve God (10:45)
- Put the needs of others first; it is doing what God asks us to do that helps others come to know God (10:45)
- Do not seek your will but God's (14:36)
- Denying self, take up your cross, and follow Jesus (Luke 9:23)

Service in Action

1. Pray and ask God to reveal someone you need to serve.
2. Ask God to bring to mind ways you can serve that person.
3. Plan what you will do, gather what is necessary to do it, and arrange a time to serve the individual.
4. Ask God to give you a servant's heart as you put the plan into action. How can you show the individual that he or she is valuable to God?
5. Record what you did, how it changed your attitudes and actions, and what happened in your relationship with the individual.

Questions

1. Name someone you classify as a great person. What characteristics made them great?

2. If you were one of the twelve disciples, how do you think you would've responded to Jesus' announcement in Mark 10:33–34? How do our motives and expectations affect our interpretation of God's word to us?

3. What do you wish God would do for you? Why? What is the motive behind your request?

4. How do people tend to define greatness in God's kingdom?

5. Whom do you find difficult to serve?

6. In your workplace or daily environment, is greatness measured by the power and position a person holds or by the quality of their character and the service they provide for others?

lesson 10

Symbolic Acts of Judgment

MAIN IDEA

Jesus cursed a fig tree and cleansed the temple, symbolizing God's judgment on Israel.

QUESTION TO EXPLORE

How spiritually fruitful is my life and the life of my church?

STUDY AIM

To evaluate the spiritual fruitfulness of my life and my church

QUICK READ

God expects fruit from his people. Jesus cursed a fig tree and cleansed the temple, symbolizing God's judgment upon Israel's fruitlessness.

Introduction

Three years ago I planted a fig tree in our yard, which quickly grew lush with leaves. But deer would eat the leaves as soon as they appeared. The tree is still struggling, and I am frustrated because it has never produced a single fig.

When Jesus cursed a fig tree and purged the temple both acts symbolized that God expected fruit from his people. He expected fruit from the tree and the temple, and when they did not produce it, judgment followed (Luke 13:6–9). These two distinct events are woven together like strands in a braid because they communicate the same message.

Jesus' time with his disciples was getting short. On Palm Sunday, Jesus rode into Jerusalem and was hailed as the messianic king (Mark 11:7–10). Late Sunday afternoon, Jesus inspected the temple area, probably looking for spiritual fruit, and then departed to spend the night in Bethany.

Mark 11:12–33

12 On the next day, when they had left Bethany, He became hungry.13 Seeing at a distance a fig tree in leaf, He went to see if perhaps He would find anything on it; and when He came to it, He found nothing but leaves, for it was not the season for figs. 14 He said to it, "May no one ever eat fruit from you again!" And His disciples were listening.

15 Then they came to Jerusalem. And He entered the temple and began to drive out those who were buying and

selling in the temple, and overturned the tables of the money changers and the seats of those who were selling doves; **16** and He would not permit anyone to carry merchandise through the temple. **17** And He began to teach and say to them, "Is it not written, 'MY HOUSE SHALL BE CALLED A HOUSE OF PRAYER FOR ALL THE NATIONS'? But you have made it a ROBBERS' DEN." **18** The chief priests and the scribes heard this, and began seeking how to destroy Him; for they were afraid of Him, for the whole crowd was astonished at His teaching.

19 When evening came, they would go out of the city.

20 As they were passing by in the morning, they saw the fig tree withered from the roots up. **21** Being reminded, Peter said to Him, "Rabbi, look, the fig tree which You cursed has withered." **22** And Jesus answered saying to them, "Have faith in God. **23** Truly I say to you, whoever says to this mountain, 'Be taken up and cast into the sea,' and does not doubt in his heart, but believes that what he says is going to happen, it will be granted him. **24** Therefore I say to you, all things for which you pray and ask, believe that you have received them, and they will be granted you.**25** Whenever you stand praying, forgive, if you have anything against anyone, so that your Father who is in heaven will also forgive you your transgressions. **26** [But if you do not forgive, neither will your Father who is in heaven forgive your transgressions."]

27 They came again to Jerusalem. And as He was walking in the temple, the chief priests and the scribes and the elders came to Him, **28** and began saying to Him, "By what authority are You doing these things, or who gave You this authority to do these things?" **29** And Jesus said to them, "I will ask you one question, and you answer Me, and then I will tell you by what authority I do these things. **30** Was the baptism of John from heaven, or from men? Answer Me." **31** They began reasoning among themselves, saying, "If we say, 'From heaven,' He will say, 'Then why did you not believe him?' **32** But shall we say, 'From men'?"—they were afraid of the people, for everyone considered John to have been a real prophet. **33** Answering Jesus, they said, "We do not know." And Jesus said to them, "Nor will I tell you by what authority I do these things."

Jesus Searched for Fruit (11:11–14)

While walking toward Jerusalem, Jesus saw in the distance a fig tree lush with leaves; however, close inspection revealed an absence of fruit. He immediately cursed it. (Although the fig harvest season was a couple of months later, some fig varieties produce small fruit from the time they sprout leaves.)

The destructive cursing of the fig tree contrasts sharply with the other miracles Jesus performed. Although some people perceive it was out of character for Jesus to expect figs out of season, three factors impacted the cursing of the tree.

1. Pragmatically and literally, Jesus did not have three months to wait for fig season. In less than a week, he would die. He needed to make his point with his disciples by using a tree that was presumed to have fruit but did not. The cursing of the fig tree is complementary to the purging of the temple. While the temple was busier than ever, there was no spiritual fruit present.

God expects our spiritual lives and religious activities to produce fruit continuously. When there is no fruit, we are not fulfilling his purposes.

2. The fig tree represented Judaism. God brought the people of Israel into existence so that through their lives others could know God (Genesis 12:3). The nation of Israel existed to produce fruit for God. Frequently in the Old Testament, the fig tree represents Israel and its fruitlessness (cf. Jeremiah 8:13; Hosea 9:10; Micah 7:1; Nahum 3:12). A fruit tree that does not produce fruit will not be cultivated, as Jesus' parable in Luke 13:6–9 illustrates.

3. The fig tree was a metaphor for the people of God; therefore, it was logical to expect fruit out of season. God expects spiritual fruit throughout the year as a daily occurrence in our lives. In John 15:1–8, Jesus used a grapevine metaphor to teach his disciples that he was the true vine, and they were the branches. This teaching makes it clear that Jesus expects his followers to produce fruit continuously. God produces fruit through us, and if God is in us, and we are in him, the fruit will ripen.

However, if we are rooted in ourselves, then we will produce the deeds of the flesh (Galatians 5:19–21). These include the hatred, jealousy, and murder the leaders of Judaism exhibited in Mark 11:18, and the malice depicted in verses 27–33.

Jesus Dramatized the Cost of Fruitlessness (11:13–21)

What limits fruitfulness for God? First, many believers today lack motivation and focus because they do not realize they must perpetually produce fruit. Active people (lots of leaves) pack the temple (the religious system), but sometimes the values of the religious system are barren (no spiritual fruit).

Also, believers often forget God desires a daily connection with him, much like branches attached to a grapevine or a fig tree. Appearing "Christian" is not enough. God is not impressed with appearances. He is looking for fruitfulness which flows from the inner life-source of an individual. When we remain connected to Jesus, and his life flows through us, we will perpetually produce spiritual fruit.

Jesus entered the temple and began to cast out those who were buying and selling in the Gentile area. Since most worshippers had to travel through the desert to the temple, their sacrifices would not meet the established quality control standards upon their arrival. Thus, the religious leaders endorsed a system of selling sacrificial animals onsite at the temple. Furthermore, they had money changers in the temple to convert other currencies into the shekels required for paying the annual temple tax. But the temple leaders positioned the animals and the exchange booths in the Gentile area, which was the only part of the temple where non-Hebrew people could legally go. The marketplace cacophony made the Gentile area difficult for the Gentiles to enter and worship God.

Jesus drove the animals, sellers, and money changers out of the temple as a visual enactment of the judgment of God upon Judaism and their barren state of worship. By doing this, Jesus pronounced their activities as contrary to God's purposes for the temple.

The temple was a house of prayer for all ethnic groups (from the Greek word *ethnos*), which included the Gentiles. By making their worship section a barn and bartering area, they undermined prayer and worship and hindered people from focusing on God.

Do churches today make it difficult for outsiders to enter and encounter God? If so, are we not also in danger of experiencing God's judgment?

Some read Mark 11:17 ("robbers den") as prohibiting business entanglements within the church, which is not bad advice. However, the emphasis here is not on robberies occurring in the building. A den is where robbers retreat after completing their dirty work. It is also where they plan future evil schemes.

Jesus made it clear that people cannot live like the devil all week, and then attend church on Sunday to appear holy. It is also sinful to corrupt a group whose purpose is to honor and reverence God. Jesus knew the chief priests and scribes were desecrating the temple for personal gain, which is why they began plotting to destroy him (11:18).

When we enter a church to worship God, we should focus on him and how to enhance our relationship with him. When our religious activities become a substitute for loving God, we are in danger of becoming a fruitless church. Some Christians spend their entire lives physically attending church, but miss the spiritual reality of God's call to each believer to impact others with his love and grace each day.

Jesus Revealed the Fruitful Connection (11:19–28)

When evening came, Jesus and the disciples left Jerusalem (11:19), presumably for Bethany. On Tuesday morning, as they headed back to Jerusalem, the disciples noticed the fig tree had withered from the roots (11:20). Peter commented to Jesus about the withered tree (11:21).

Jesus responded with four simple words" "Have faith in God" (11:22).

With the awareness that his actions and words depicted the impending destruction of Jerusalem and the temple (Mark 13:2; Luke 19:42–44), Jesus communicated that his followers must root their salvation and faith in God, not earthly settings. The Romans would lay siege to Jerusalem and destroy the city and the temple, but faith in God would stand forever.

By faith, we remain connected to God (Mark 11:22–23), who then produces fruit through us. Fruitfulness also comes as we pray for God's will to be done, believing that he has already taken action regarding what he has led us to pray (11:24). Practicing forgiveness also produces fruit (11:25). Whether as individuals or as a church, we need to forgive one another and release those who hurt us into the care of God. John 15:1–8 reveals other factors vital to fruit production.

Implications and Actions

God expects his followers to remain spiritually vibrant and fruitful. The cursed fig tree looked alive but was barren of life-giving fruit. Far too often religious systems lose their way and fail to connect people to the life of God.

As followers of Christ, we should regularly evaluate our lives and churches to ensure spiritual vitality and nourishment for others. Fruitfulness comes naturally when the Spirit of God flows through us. We need to make sure that our relationship with Christ is constant, consistent, and communicated. Faith must remain rooted in God, not human systems. God expects fruit in us and from us. He also expects fruit in and through our churches.

Are we producing the fruit that feeds those hungry for God?

Improving Fruitfulness

God expects fruit (something tangible and spiritually nourishing for others) from you and your church. How can you practically evaluate and improve the spiritual fruitfulness of your life and that of your church?

Use each of the characteristics of the fruit of the Spirit listed in Galatians 5:22–23 to examine your attitudes, character, and behaviors to see if these are present in your life and your church's activities.

"... The fruit of the Spirit is ..."

- Love: loving, putting others' needs before mine
- Joy: joyful, happily content
- Peace: whole, complete, not striving
- Patience: long-suffering, slow to take offense
- Kindness: compassionate action
- Goodness: moral, ethical
- Faithfulness: trusting, committed, reliable
- Gentleness: humble, respecting life's fragility
- Self-control: disciplined, able to restrain self in speech and behavior

Example:

1. Am I loving? Are we as a church loving?
2. How can I become more loving? How can our church become more loving?

Fruitful Guidance from John 15:4–8

- Live in constant interaction with God (John 15:4).
- Abide in God, who gives life to us and produces fruit through us (15:4).
- When God is in us and his life flows out of us, we bear much fruit (15:5).
- As we abide in God and his truth, we will pray for God's will to be done, and he will do it (15:7).
- God gets the glory from fruit produced through us, and such fruit identifies us as his disciples (15:8).

Questions

1. If Jesus were to inspect your life would he find fruit? Do your attitudes, behavior, and activities reveal to others that God is alive and active in your life?

2. Is there evidence that God is working in and through your church? Does your church have values, attitudes, and relationships noticeably different from secular clubs or social groups?

3. Is your faith rooted in God, or is it rooted in your feelings or the people or events of your church? Is your church convincing people of God's greatness, or has the focus become more about how great your church is?

4. Do you spend time each day reading the Bible, listening to what God is saying about your life, and what he wants to do in and through you? Do you stay connected to God by prayerfully interacting with him throughout the day, by conversing with him, and recognizing where he is at work?

5. Do you live as one who realizes God is evaluating your spiritual life for fruit that gives life to others? Are you living your life as one who understands that God expects your life to produce fruit that gives samples of God's reality, life, and values to the people you encounter?

lesson  11

Predictions, Promises, and Pride

MAIN IDEA

As Jesus inaugurated a new covenant, his followers responded with betrayal and misguided pride.

QUESTION TO EXPLORE

How can we avoid spiritual pride and betrayal?

STUDY AIM

To consider how I can avoid spiritual pride and betrayal

QUICK READ

Jesus instituted the tradition of the Lord's Supper as a symbol of his personal sacrifice and to represent the commitment of his disciples' love and loyalty. But in the same room and at the same time, betrayal and spiritual pride were present.

Introduction

The Lord's Supper is a tradition Christians have observed from the time Jesus gathered his disciples in the Upper Room. When Roman-era Christians faced persecution in the second and third centuries, they huddled together in the catacombs under the city and whispered, "Do this in remembrance of me." In the Middle Ages, when Christendom was the law of the land, the masses flowed into the great cathedrals, took the bread, and said, "the body of Christ."

In the nineteenth-century American South, dark woods may have hidden faithful slaves illegally gathered for worship around a fire. Perhaps they softly sang a hymn and then drank freely from the cup of freedom found in the blood of Christ, which symbolized a new covenant. When we take the Lord's Supper in our churches today, it is nothing new, nor is it done in isolation. We are the latest believers in a long line of believers that began with Jesus.[1]

Mark 14:12–31

12 On the first day of the Feast of Unleavened Bread, when it was customary to sacrifice the Passover lamb, Jesus' disciples asked him, "Where do you want us to go and make preparations for you to eat the Passover?"

13 So he sent two of his disciples, telling them, "Go into the city, and a <u>man</u> carrying a jar of water will meet you. Follow

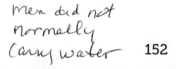
men did not
normally
carry water

him. **14** Say to the owner of the house he enters, 'The Teacher asks: Where is my guest room, where I may eat the Passover with my disciples?' **15** He will show you a large upper room, furnished and ready. Make preparations for us there."

16 The disciples left, went into the city and found things just as Jesus had told them. So they prepared the Passover.

17 When evening came, Jesus arrived with the Twelve. **18** While they were reclining at the table eating, he said, "I tell you the truth, one of you will betray me—one who is eating with me."

19 They were saddened, and one by one they said to him, "Surely not I?"

20 "It is one of the Twelve," he replied, "one who dips bread into the bowl with me.

21 The Son of Man will go just as it is written about him. But woe to that man who betrays the Son of Man! It would be better for him if he had not been born."

22 While they were eating, Jesus took bread, gave thanks and broke it, and gave it to his disciples, saying, "Take it; this is my body."

23 Then he took the cup, gave thanks and offered it to them, and they all drank from it.

24 "This is my blood of the covenant, which is poured out for many," he said to them. **25** "I tell you the truth, I will not drink again of the fruit of the vine until that day when I drink it anew in the kingdom of God."

26 When they had sung a hymn, they went out to the Mount of Olives.

27 "You will all fall away," Jesus told them, "for it is written:

"'I will strike the shepherd,
    and the sheep will be scattered.'

28 But after I have risen, I will go ahead of you into Galilee."

29 Peter declared, "Even if all fall away, I will not."

30 "I tell you the truth," Jesus answered, "today—yes, tonight—before the rooster crows twice you yourself will disown me three times."

31 But Peter insisted emphatically, "Even if I have to die with you, I will never disown you." And all the others said the same.

Love and Betrayal (14:1–10)

Mark 14 recounts the story for us. It was Passover week, and Jesus and his disciples had been staying in Bethany, just outside of Jerusalem. Bethany was the home of Mary, Martha, and Lazarus. Mark tells us Jesus was eating at the home of a man named Simon when a woman entered and anointed the head of Jesus with expensive perfume. The Gospel of John tells a similar story and identifies the woman as Mary, the sister of Martha and Lazarus. Jesus accepted this gift as an act of love and devotion, this anointing foreshadowing the preparation for his burial.

In the midst of this tender act of love, evil was active. Judas and the chief priests were plotting Jesus' arrest. Intertwined in this story were both love and betrayal.

Saved by the Blood of the Lamb (14:12)

It is significant that the Book of Mark reveals that it was the day of the Feast of Unleavened Bread and the time for the sacrifice of the Passover Lamb, which recalls the enslave-ment of the Hebrews in Egypt. Moses asked the Pharaoh to set the people free. Pharaoh refused to grant the Hebrews freedom, even after enduring terrible plagues. God, how-ever, wanted his people set free. The sudden death of all of the firstborn sons of Egypt was the final plague.

God told the Hebrew people to take an unblemished lamb, sacrifice it, and smear its blood on their doors. When the angel of death came and saw the blood of the lamb on a door, he would "pass over" that house and death would not enter that home. The blood of the lamb saved them.

Moses told the Israelites to celebrate this great salva-tion event by sacrificing a lamb in the temple for the sins of the people. Also, they were to prepare a feast without using yeast. The Feast of Unleavened Bread was the meal Jesus instructed his disciples to prepare in Jerusalem.

Preparations and Predictions (14:13–21)

Jesus gave two disciples specific instructions concerning the preparation for the feast. He told them whom to meet, what to ask, and what they would find. Some people view Jesus' foreknowledge of the event as miraculous. How did Jesus know they would find a man carrying water? How did he know there would be an upstairs room prepared? Perhaps this was supernatural knowledge; however, it is not neces-sarily so. It is possible prior arrangements were made, and

Mark did not record it. Either way, the disciples obediently prepared for the meal.

A shared meal is more than a way to satisfy an appetite. Today, when we share a meal with someone, it offers an opportunity for fellowship and friendship. Wednesday night meals at church and potluck suppers are more than convenient ways to feed busy families. They are opportunities for Christian fellowship.

In Jesus' day, a shared meal was a bond, a symbol of love and friendship. Eating with someone was a pledge of loyalty. No wonder it was such a shock when Jesus announced that one of the men eating at that table would betray him. To betray someone with whom you had shared a meal was unthinkable. However, Jesus said that right in the middle of the family meal which symbolized love and loyalty, betrayal was also present at the table.

The disciples did not know it at the time, but before the meal, Judas had been plotting with the chief priests. Judas betrayed Jesus—and all of the disciples. You see the resentment of the betrayal in the pages of the New Testament. A reminder of his betrayal of the Lord is always attached to his name. Judas ate with them, and then betrayed them all.

Judas' betrayal did not come as a surprise to Jesus. Jesus knew prophecies that spoke of the betrayal of the Messiah. His awareness did not negate the seriousness of the matter, however. There are always grave consequences to sin and betrayal.

Judas may be the most notorious of sinners, but in truth, he is not alone. We all have betrayed Jesus and one another. We are all sinners. Betrayal comes in all shapes and sizes. Maybe it is an occasional "white lie" or a whisper of gossip. Maybe it is a broken trust, an unfaithful moment, or an untimely word that pierces someone's heart. Judas may be the most notorious betrayer, but he is not alone. We, too, betray Jesus and one another.

It is ironic that loyalty and betrayal, along with kinship and treachery, existed in the same room at the same time. It happens in church sometimes. We gather for worship and take the Lord's Supper. It is a symbol of community, family, and sacrifice, yet we take the Supper with a person against whom we hold resentment or hatred. In the same room and at the same time we eat with brothers and sisters, yet harbor betrayal in our hearts. It is part of the human condition; good and evil are mixed up in the same bowl of stew.

Provision and Community (14:22–26)

Thankfully there is a remedy for the sinful nature of the human condition: the body and blood of Christ. Jesus knew he would die for the sins of the world. The next day, he would hang on a cross for all who betray him.

In the midst of the Passover meal, Jesus took bread, gave thanks, broke it, and gave it to his disciples. "This is my body," he said to them. Some misunderstand what Jesus meant when he declared the bread to be his body, thinking the bread literally became the body of Christ. Baptists have always insisted on the symbolic nature of Jesus' words, knowing that symbolism does not weaken the meaning of the Supper.

The same is true of the cup. Jesus declared it to be the blood of the covenant. Again, he was speaking symbolically. With the cup, Jesus declared that a relationship with God was no longer dependent upon the sacrifice of animals in the temple. The sacrifice of Jesus is the basis of a relationship with God. With the death, burial, and resurrection of Jesus, a new age began.

The Bible notes that Jesus and the disciples drank from a common cup, even Judas. Jesus knew his betrayer, but he did not exclude Judas from participating in the Supper. Even at the last minute, Judas could have lived up to the commitment of loyalty symbolized in this common meal. Instead, he chose betrayal.

When Christians take the Lord's Supper today, it continues to be heavy with meaning. First, the elements of Holy Communion force us to look back at the sacrifice Jesus made. It is difficult to eat the bread and not think about Jesus' broken body. It is hard to taste the red juice and forget that he shed blood for our sins. The Lord's Supper takes us back to the cross.

However, the Lord's Supper also helps us look forward. Jesus looked forward to the day when he will again drink from the fruit of the vine; God's salvation plan will be complete, and we all will gather around a heavenly table for the

Messianic feast. The Lord's Supper is merely a foretaste of glory to come.

Likewise, the Lord's Supper makes us look inward. When we take Holy Communion, we should remember the betrayal that was in the room that night long ago. Taking the Supper ought to make all of us aware that we are capable of betrayal. We, too, should pose the question each disciple asked, "Surely not I?"

The Lord's Supper should also make us look around. We do not take it in a social vacuum. We take it with other brothers and sisters who are part of the body of Christ we call the church. As we take Holy Communion, we do so in a community, and we recognize that taking it with others symbolizes the love and loyalty we have for one another.

Promises and Pride (14:27–31)

Jesus knew that even after that special meal of love and loyalty, his disciples would continue to struggle in their commitment to him. Jesus predicted that all of his disciples would abandon him. Jesus quoted Zechariah 13:7 as prophetic evidence of this abandonment. Even so, his prediction contained an element of hope promising resurrection and a future meeting with them.

The disciples did not seem to understand what Jesus was saying. Even after spending three years with Jesus, it was difficult for them to see how prophecy applied to current events.

Peter took exception to Jesus' prediction of abandonment. Spiritual pride may have made him overconfident. He did not doubt that the other disciples might abandon Jesus, but he was confident of his loyalty. As later events proved, he was wrong.

Jesus was not surprised. He predicted Peter would disavow him three times before morning. Peter swore to the contrary; however, that was easy to say in the safe confines of the Upper Room. Peter did another kind of swearing later, around a fire in the courtyard when circumstances were not so safe. Peter was not the only one to fail Jesus that night. All the disciples swore allegiance in the Upper Room. Later, when things got rough, they were nowhere to be found.

Implications and Actions

Christians today are often tempted to look at the actions of Judas and the attitude of Peter and think they would never respond in a similar manner. How could Judas have eaten the Lord's Supper with betrayal in his heart? How could Peter have sworn his allegiance to Jesus and within a few hours deny he knew him, not once but three times? In hindsight, it seems incredible. But even now, we are equally capable of betrayal and spiritual pride. We sit down in church and take the Lord's Supper with our brothers and sisters. We remember the sacrifice Jesus made. We look forward to the great feast in heaven. We pledge ourselves to Jesus and one another. However, as soon as we get out of the safe confines of the church walls, we betray Jesus and one another with our attitudes and actions.

It is a reminder that even now we are filled with loyalty and betrayal, kinship and treachery. Love and betrayal intertwine everyone's story. They are part of the human condition. Thankfully, there is a remedy for the conundrum. When we participate in the Lord's Supper, we can be reminded anew of the body and blood of Christ. Jesus died for our sins.

The Passover Meal

Jews still celebrate the Passover meal today. It is called the Seder and marks the beginning of the Passover season, celebrated in late March and early April. The meal involves four glasses of wine with symbolic meaning, unleavened bread called "matzah," bitter herbs, a meat (often lamb), and other dishes with symbolic meaning. During the meal, the story of the Exodus from Egypt is told to the children so they will never forget how God saved his people.

Jesus and his disciples were eating the Passover meal in the Upper Room. Jesus gave the meal extra meaning with the introduction of what we now call the Lord's Supper.

An Unworthy Manner

The Apostle Paul discussed the Lord's Supper in 1 Corinthians 11:17–34. In verse 27, Paul said, "whoever eats the bread or drinks the cup of the Lord in an unworthy manner will be guilty of sinning against the body and blood of the Lord." In light of this lesson and the context of Paul's discussion, what do you think he meant?

Questions

1. Baptists believe the Lord's Supper is a symbolic representation of the body and blood of Christ. Does the symbolic nature of the elements add or subtract from the meaning of the Supper?

2. What are ways you have betrayed Christ even though you have pledged to be loyal to him?

3. Think about the last time you took the Lord's Supper. Were there people in your church with whom you had a strained relationship? Are there people whom you cannot forgive? Does taking the Supper with them have any bearing on your attitude toward them?

4. In what areas do you struggle with spiritual pride?

5. If your church never celebrated the Lord's Supper, would that make any difference to you? Why or why not?

Notes

1. Unless otherwise indicated, all Scripture quotations in lessons 11–13 and the Christmas lesson are from the New International Version (1984 edition).

lesson 12

Betrayed, Arrested, and Tried

MAIN IDEA

Jesus endured his betrayal, arrest, and trials with uncommon grace and humility.

QUESTION TO EXPLORE

When placed under pressure, how can we imitate Jesus' example of grace and humility?

STUDY AIM

To respond to trials with grace and humility

QUICK READ

The betrayal, arrest, and trials of Jesus revealed his total commitment to following the will of God. Jesus' response of grace and humility proved he was faithful to God rather than his own self-interest.

Introduction

The distinguished Italian artist Caravaggio depicted the moment of Jesus' betrayal in the dark painting usually entitled *The Kiss of Judas*. The painting pictures Judas grasping onto Jesus and planting a kiss on him while Roman soldiers grasp his clothes to arrest him. The characters in the painting point to the themes found in this lesson.

There is Judas, of course. Judas betrayed Jesus with a symbol of friendship and loyalty. On the right side of the painting, light shines on the face of a pursuer, and art historians are certain it is a self-portrait of the artist, who inserted his image as if to say he was part of the betrayal of Christ. To the left of Jesus, a man is running away in horror, a picture of disciples abandoning Jesus in his hour of greatest distress.

But Jesus is the focal point of the painting. His face depicts humble resignation as if to say he is ready to surrender to the will of God. His hands are gently folded in front of him, void of self-defense or resistance. He is ready to do God's will with grace and humility.

Mark 14:43–52

43 Just as he was speaking, Judas, one of the Twelve, appeared. With him was a crowd armed with swords and clubs, sent from the chief priests, the teachers of the law, and the elders.

44 Now the betrayer had arranged a signal with them: "The one I kiss is the man; arrest him and lead him away under guard." **45** Going at once to Jesus, Judas said, "Rabbi!" and kissed him. **46** The men seized Jesus and arrested him. **47** Then one of those standing near drew his sword and struck the servant of the high priest, cutting off his ear.

48 "Am I leading a rebellion," said Jesus, "that you have come out with swords and clubs to capture me? **49** Every day I was with you, teaching in the temple courts, and you did not arrest me. But the Scriptures must be fulfilled." **50** Then everyone deserted him and fled.

51 A young man, wearing nothing but a linen garment, was following Jesus. When they seized him, **52** he fled naked, leaving his garment behind.

Mark 15:1–15

1 Very early in the morning, the chief priests, with the elders, the teachers of the law and the whole Sanhedrin, reached a decision. They bound Jesus, led him away and handed him over to Pilate.

2 "Are you the king of the Jews?" asked Pilate.

"Yes, it is as you say," Jesus replied.

3 The chief priests accused him of many things. **4** So again Pilate asked him, "Aren't you going to answer? See how many things they are accusing you of."

5 But Jesus still made no reply, and Pilate was amazed.

6 Now it was the custom at the Feast to release a prisoner whom the people requested. **7** A man called Barabbas was in prison with the insurrectionists who had committed murder in the uprising. [8] The crowd came up and asked Pilate to do for them what he usually did.

[9] "Do you want me to release to you the king of the Jews?" asked Pilate, [10] knowing it was out of envy that the chief priests had handed Jesus over to him. [11] But the chief priests stirred up the crowd to have Pilate release Barabbas instead.

[12] "What shall I do, then, with the one you call the king of the Jews?" Pilate asked them.

[13] "Crucify him!" they shouted.

[14] "Why? What crime has he committed?" asked Pilate.

But they shouted all the louder, "Crucify him!"

[15] Wanting to satisfy the crowd, Pilate released Barabbas to them. He had Jesus flogged, and handed him over to be crucified.

Kissed in the Dark (14:43–52)

After eating the Passover meal, Jesus led his disciples to the Garden of Gethsemane, where he prayed in agony, knowing the trial that was coming. He asked his disciples to watch and pray with him, but already their resolve was waning, and they abandoned him for sleep.

Jesus prayed for another path, but there was no other way. Determined to follow the will of God, he cast aside personal well-being and responded with grace and humility to the events that would follow.

Judas arrived with an armed mob sent by the Jewish authorities. Presumably, they felt the need to arm themselves because of the popular misconception that Jesus was trying to lead a revolt against the earthly powers.

The kiss of Judas is the most famous kiss in history. Judas prearranged the signal. We might assume that everyone would have recognized Jesus on sight, but obviously, that was not the case. In a day without photography or newscasts, there were many people who did not recognize Jesus. The arresters needed to ensure they had the right man.

Judas went directly to Jesus and greeted him with a term of respect, "Rabbi!" Then, he kissed him. In many cultures, a kiss is a normal greeting even if you are greeting someone of the same gender. A kiss is a mark of friendship, a sign of devotion and loyalty. But just as a double agent in a spy novel kisses the man marked for death, the kiss of Judas was not a sign of loyalty or love; it was a signal for betrayal.

Judas feigned friendship to identify Jesus to his enemies. Judas' love was feigned—a visible expression of tenderness that cloaked a hard, deceitful heart. There is nothing worse than the betrayal of a friend. You expect betrayal from an enemy. But when someone you trust stabs you in the back, it hurts deeply. The kiss of Judas led to a series of reactions. The first and most obvious was the arrest of Jesus. As soon as the armed mob knew they had the right man, they grabbed him.

Peter's reaction, though well-meaning, was not helpful. He picked up a sword and cut off the ear of a servant of the High Priest. The Book of Mark does not tell us it was Peter, but John's Gospel does. We could have probably guessed it was Peter even if John had not told us. Peter often reacted in haste and without forethought. His violent reaction inadvertently played into the plan of the enemy, giving the mob an excuse for more violence.

The other disciples reacted differently; they abandoned Jesus. Jesus correctly predicted his "sheep" would scatter. Mark recorded the only account of a mysterious young man running away naked. Some have speculated that Mark was that man. Although his identity cannot be confirmed, the young man's retreat symbolizes the total abandonment of Jesus.

Jesus demonstrated a different reaction. He did not respond with violence. In fact, Jesus challenged the violent actions of the mob by denying any intention of rebellion. Nor did Jesus respond by running away. We know from his desperate prayer in the garden that he dreaded this moment. But Jesus responded with grace and humility because he knew that he must fulfill the Scriptures. He submitted to the will of the Father rather than seeking self-preservation.

Trial and Denial (14:53–72)

After his arrest, Jesus stood trial before the Sanhedrin. The Sanhedrin, the Jewish governing council, had considerable power in local matters, but they did not have authority to sentence a person to death. Later, as we will see, they took Jesus to the Roman governor Pilate and influenced him to carry out their plan.

The Sanhedrin convicted Jesus of blasphemy. The testimony of witnesses seemed less than trustworthy, but some evidence indicated that Jesus had threatened to destroy the temple. Obviously, those witnesses did not understand Jesus or his mission.

Jesus finally affirmed that he was the Christ and asserted his heavenly authority. This confession was all the Sanhedrin needed to hear. Blasphemy was a crime worthy of death.

In the meantime, Peter, who had been so bold in the garden, wilted under the heat of pressure. When confronted by a servant girl, Peter did not stand up for Jesus. Three times he denied knowing Jesus. Peter had sworn he would never deny Jesus, but he did. It was not surprising; Jesus had predicted the denials, but they must have felt like stabs in his back.

Questioned and Condemned (15:1–15)

When morning came, the Sanhedrin sent Jesus to Pilate. Pilate was the Roman governor who was in Jerusalem during the Passover. He did not care about the religious nature of the Passover observance but was there because of the political problems that could arise amidst such a large gathering. He was concerned about a possible revolt and was prepared to squash any riots or disturbances. This concern played into the hands of the Sanhedrin.

Pilate had a difficult relationship with the Jewish people. He had no qualms about shedding Jewish blood. He took office in 26 A.D. and spent much of his time finding ways to oppress the people he ruled. Later, he was removed from his position because of a brutal incident involving a group of Samaritans.

It is somewhat surprising that the Sanhedrin went to Pilate, considering their strained relationship. Their strategy seemed to involve convincing Pilate that Jesus posed a political threat. After all, Jesus was always talking about a new kingdom. The leaders of the Sanhedrin knew Pilate would be ready to put down any insurrection.

Pilate asked Jesus if he was the King of the Jews. It was a political question. He wanted to know if Jesus was planning an insurrection.

Jesus' answer was ambiguous. In the NIV, Jesus answered in the affirmative; however, other translations are closer to the real meaning. "That is what you say," may be a better interpretation. In one sense, Jesus was not King of the Jews. He was not pretending to sit on a Jewish throne in the way Pilate was implying. However, in another sense, Jesus is the King of the Jews and everyone else!

Pilate was unconvinced of Jesus' guilt. Even when the chief priests continued to accuse Jesus, and he refused to defend himself, Pilate could see through their plot. He knew the only reason the Jewish leaders were accusing Jesus was that they envied his popular support. Pilate was not concerned with internal Jewish religious squabbles. He was only concerned with quelling civil unrest.

Pilate was amazed Jesus did not defend himself. Most people in Jesus' situation would scream their innocence. However, Jesus was resigned to the fact that what was happening was part of God's plan. This awareness allowed Jesus, and later his followers, to respond to adversity with grace and humility.

Pilate was not opposed to offending the Jews. He did so with regularity. But he also had enough political sense to know he had to throw them a bone sometimes to calm any thought of civil unrest. One of the ways he did that was to release a prisoner the people requested each year at the Passover feast. Pilate saw this as an opportunity to release Jesus, whom he regarded as no real threat to the civil authorities.

The chief priests stirred up the people to ask for Barabbas instead. Pilate would have been more reluctant to release Barabbas because the man actually was a threat to the authorities. He was involved in a previous deadly insurrection against the Romans. Barabbas was a criminal who truly did raise concern in the Roman government.

The people wanted Jesus crucified, and Barabbas released. It is impossible to know if the crowd was made up of the same individuals who had shouted "Hosanna!" when Jesus rode into town a few days earlier, but it is hard to miss the irony of the sudden change of heart among the inhabitants of Jerusalem.

Finally, Pilate agreed to turn Jesus over for crucifixion. He calculated the political risk and decided the politically correct thing to do was to surrender to the will of the crowd. He could not afford to start a riot. He was already skating on thin ice with his superiors, and he did not want to make matters worse. Pilate saved himself by condemning the one person who could save him. Once again, Jesus was rejected.

Implications and Actions

As Christians, we commit to follow and imitate Jesus. But all of us have found it difficult to react with Christ-like grace and humility when faced with trials and tribulations. Sometimes, we are tempted to fight back. Sometimes, we just run away from Jesus and hide in dark places.

Jesus provided an example of how to respond to pressure with grace and humility. He had a clear understanding of God's will and was willing to put aside his well-being for the sake of God's plan. A clear understanding of Scripture provides us with a sense of God's plan. Demonstrating grace and humility when we face trials does not signify weakness. These are signs of strength when our commitment to God's will is greater than our allegiance to our well-being. If we keep God's plan in mind, we can face trials with the grace and humility of Jesus.

A Look at Pontius Pilate

Pilate was appointed the governor of Judea by the Roman government in 26 A.D. He was a contemporary with Sejanus in Rome and Flaccus in Egypt, leaders who were pursuing policies focused on the destruction of the Jewish people. Pilate followed the same types of policies in Judea.

Pilate often provoked the Jews. For example, he brought into Jerusalem military symbols bearing the image of Caesar in defiance of Jewish law. He was finally forced to remove them when Jews offered to die at the hands of his soldiers rather than submit to such blasphemy. Pilate often suppressed protests by planting soldiers in plain clothing among Jewish crowds. These soldiers may have murdered protesters. Luke 13:1 reads, "The Galileans whose blood Pilate had mingled with their sacrifice." Pilate was a ruthless man.

Roman leaders removed Pilate from his position when people protested his attack on some Samaritan worshipers who were attending an event on Mount Gerizim, their holy mountain. After returning to Rome to account for his actions, he disappeared from the annals of history.

Case Study

John is a Sunday School teacher in his church. One of the members of his class started an untrue rumor that has damaged John's reputation. What are some ways John could react to this insult? How would Jesus respond?

Questions

1. What are some ways Christians betray Jesus in the guise of friendship and loyalty?

2. Think of ways you have responded to trials and pressure in the past. Did you fight? Did you run? What would Jesus have done in those situations?

3. How can you discern God's will? How did Jesus know it was God's will for him to face the trials he faced?

4. Why do you think Pilate decided to crucify Jesus even though he knew Jesus was innocent? Name some examples of how people surrender to pressure or self-interest instead of doing the right thing.

5. How can you face insult and injury with grace and humility?

lesson  13

Death is Defeated!

MAIN IDEA

Jesus' death and resurrection paved the way for our salvation.

QUESTIONS TO EXPLORE

Have I placed my faith in Jesus? How can the details of Jesus' death and resurrection inspire me to live for him?

STUDY AIM

To place my faith in Jesus and be inspired to live for him

QUICK READ

The suffering of Jesus on the cross provides a path for the forgiveness of sin. The resurrection of Jesus provides hope for a new life. In light of his death and resurrection, we can place our faith in him and live our lives for him.

Introduction

A cross hangs on the back wall of our church's baptistry. One of the men in our church made it. It is a beautiful work of art, backlit so it stands out against the wall behind it. When someone is baptized, the cross symbolizes how we are crucified with Christ and buried by baptism into death with him.

In reality, there is nothing beautiful about a crucifixion. It was a gruesome, bloody, violent event. The Jewish historian Josephus wrote that crucifixion is "the most wretched of all ways of dying."[1] The Roman orator Cicero said, "Even the mere word, cross, must remain far not only from the lips of the citizens of Rome, but also from their thoughts, their eyes, and their ears."[2]

The crucifixion of Jesus was gruesome. We have romanticized the cross in modern times; cleaned it up so we can put it on our steeples and wear it around our necks without frightening people. Perhaps our romantic version of the cross has blanketed the scandal. The cross is an important symbol for Christians, but we must not allow our cleaned up crosses to detract from its wretchedness.

Without the brutality of the cross, there would be no hope of salvation. Without the cross, there would be no resurrection. The death and resurrection of Jesus give us the hope of eternal life.

Mark 15:33–41

33 At the sixth hour darkness came over the whole land until the ninth hour. **34** And at the ninth hour Jesus cried out in a loud voice, "Eloi, Eloi, lama sabachthani?"—which means, "My God, my God, why have you forsaken me?"

35 When some of those standing near heard this, they said, "Listen, he's calling Elijah."

36 One man ran, filled a sponge with wine vinegar, put it on a stick, and offered it to Jesus to drink. "Now leave him alone. Let's see if Elijah comes to take him down," he said.

37 With a loud cry, Jesus breathed his last.

38 The curtain of the temple was torn in two from top to bottom. **39** And when the centurion, who stood there in front of Jesus, heard his cry and saw how he died, he said, "Surely this man was the Son of God!"

40 Some women were watching from a distance. Among them were Mary Magdalene, Mary the mother of James the younger and of Joses, and Salome. **41** In Galilee these women had followed him and cared for his needs. Many other women who had come up with him to Jerusalem were also there.

Mark 16:1–8

1 When the Sabbath was over, Mary Magdalene, Mary the mother of James, and Salome bought spices so that they might go to anoint Jesus' body. **2** Very early on the first day of the week, just after sunrise, they were on their way to the tomb **3** and they asked each other, "Who will roll the stone away from the entrance of the tomb?"

4 But when they looked up, they saw that the stone, which was very large, had been rolled away. **5** As they entered the tomb, they saw a young man dressed in a white robe sitting on the right side, and they were alarmed.

6 "Don't be alarmed," he said. "You are looking for Jesus the Nazarene, who was crucified. He has risen! He is not here. See the place where they laid him. **7** But go, tell his disciples and Peter, 'He is going ahead of you into Galilee. There you will see him, just as he told you.' "

8 Trembling and bewildered, the women went out and fled from the tomb. They said nothing to anyone, because they were afraid.

The Crucifixion of Christ (15:21–32)

The background Scripture sets the scene for the death of Jesus. After Pilate had condemned Jesus, he was flogged without mercy and mocked by the soldiers in charge. Then, he began stumbling forward to Golgotha. On the way, a man named Simon of Cyrene was forced to help carry Jesus' cross to the place of execution.

When the parade reached "the place of the skull," Jesus was offered a mixture of wine and myrrh as a mild anesthetic. He refused it.

Then the Book of Mark says, "And they crucified him." The author could have said much more about this gruesome method of execution. But the terseness of the sentence needs no elaboration.

The indignity of crucifixion was not enough punishment for those who hated Jesus. He was mocked and insulted by almost everyone around him. A placard placed on the cross mocked his offense: "The King of the Jews." A thief crucified with him insulted him. Passersby hurled hurtful words. Religious leaders made fun of him. No glory was present at the cross.

The Death of Christ (15:33–41)

The Book of Mark tells us Jesus was crucified around nine in the morning. Crucifixion was a long process that took hours, often days. Jesus would only hang on his cross for six hours.

Around noon that day, the world went dark. It is impossible to know exactly what happened. Was there an eclipse? Did a sudden storm cloud block out the sun? People have speculated on various theories. It does not matter what natural phenomenon caused the world to go dark. Mark does not share this information as a weather report. The world went dark because Jesus, the light of the world, was being snuffed out.

Darkness is often a sign of judgment in the Bible. In this case, God's judgment was poured out onto his Son. Jesus took the condemnation of the world on his shoulders, even though he was innocent.

It is no wonder Jesus cried out with words of abandonment. His disciples had abandoned him, and at the moment of death and ultimate judgment he cried, "My God, my God, why have you forsaken me?" This statement is a quotation from Psalm 22:1. Some scholars say that by quoting the first verse of Psalm 22, Jesus was alluding to the complete psalm, which ends with a note of triumph and trust. It is possible. However, the theme of abandonment runs throughout this story, and the ultimate abandonment is abandonment by God. By quoting the first line of this psalm, Jesus was expressing the ultimate agony. As Jesus took on the sin of all humanity, his Father had to turn away.

Obviously, God the Father did not abandon Jesus. Nor does God abandon us when life seems dark. The cross reminds us that when it is darkest, God is working his hardest. It is hard to see God when it is dark; however, he is working nonetheless.

The people around Jesus misunderstood what Jesus had said. Some of them thought he was calling out for Elijah the prophet. The misunderstanding reflected a popular belief that Elijah often came to help people who were in distress. Those entertained by his suffering used Jesus' cry of agony to mock him all the more.

Jesus died after six hours of suffering. The Book of Mark gives us no details. There is nothing about the sword piercing his side, or water and blood flowing from his wound. Mark leaves those details for others. Mark simply communicates that Jesus cried out and breathed his last.

The effect of Jesus' death produced a new way to relate to God. The curtain in the temple tore in two from top to bottom. God took the initiative to have a relationship with us through the death of Jesus.

The curtain in the temple separated the Holy Place from the Holy of Holies. The Holy of Holies once contained the Ark of the Covenant, although by Jesus' day the Ark was probably destroyed. Once a year, the High Priest entered the Holy of Holies through the temple curtain to enter into the presence of God and offer sacrifices for the people. The rending of the curtain symbolized access to God by faith rather than by a priest. Because of the cross, all people can have a direct relationship with God.

Salvation through Jesus Christ is available to all people. Mark demonstrates this truth with the vocal response of a Roman centurion. He recognized Jesus as the Son of God. Throughout the Book of Mark, the big question has been "Who is Jesus?" The Jewish religious leaders were wrong. Judas was wrong. Even Jesus' disciples did not really get it. However, a Gentile soldier finally understood who Jesus was. The cross offers salvation to everyone.

Not everyone abandoned Jesus; some women remained faithful. In Jesus' day, women were oppressed and not viewed as reliable witnesses. But these faithful women would be at the empty tomb and become the first witnesses for Jesus. God used unlikely people to witness his greatest work.

The Resurrection of Christ (16:1–8)

Joseph of Arimathea, a member of the Sanhedrin, buried Jesus in a tomb cut out of a rock. It is surprising to learn Joseph was sympathetic to Jesus. Evidently the Jewish council was not unanimous in its condemnation of Jesus. The women who were at the cross were also present when the tomb was sealed with a large stone. They had seen the dead body of Jesus. In their eyes, hope had died with him.

Early in the morning after the Sabbath Day, the hopeless women came to the tomb to finish the task of taking care of Jesus' dead body. After what they had seen and experienced, they had no reason to hope. They had seen Jesus hanging on the cross. They had been there when his body was placed in the tomb. They knew the enemy of death firsthand— the grave swallows up life and hope. They did not even have much hope of getting into the grave with the large stone rolled across it.

Everyone can identify with hopelessness. After what we have seen and experienced, we have good reason to feel hopeless. We live in a world of perpetual war, horrible diseases, and an upside-down value system. On a personal level, you may not care that the economy is better if you do not have any money. You can find no hope in the fact that medical science has extended life expectancy if someone you love has died. There are things in this world that drain hope out of us. But we cannot live without it.

The resurrection of Jesus matters because it gives us hope. The women went to the tomb that morning without hope, but when they got there, they discovered something they did not expect. Someone had rolled away the massive stone. They did not know what had happened, but they entered the tomb.

The stone was not rolled from the tomb so Jesus could get out. God overcame death; a simple stone could not hold Jesus. The stone was rolled away so the women could get in. Inside the tomb, they would discover what happened. Inside the tomb, a place that normally holds death, they found life.

When they entered the tomb, the women saw a young man dressed in white who was the first to announce the good news. Each Gospel account gives a slightly different version of the event. The Book of Mark mentions a single young man inside the tomb. Other Gospels mention two individuals identified as angels. Each Gospel writer gives a perspective of what the women saw. But the point was not who was there; the point was who was *not* there. Jesus was not there!

In the Book of Mark, the young man told the women not to fear. Fear is the natural response when we see the unexpected. But then, the man spoke a message that could have relieved all their fears. "He has risen! He is not here." This message of good news did not immediately alleviate the fears of the women. The shock of the unexpected was still too much to grasp. However, the message was clear: the crucified Christ had risen from the dead.

The young man gave the women an assignment. They were to go back and tell the good news to the others. The culture at that time did not view women as reliable witnesses. They could not testify in court. But God chose women to be the first to tell the good news of the resurrection.

The Book of Mark ends with the women still bewildered and afraid. We know from the other Gospels that the good news did spread, and soon everyone was filled with joy. Jesus appeared to other disciples after the resurrection, and they told the world what they had seen. Hopelessness transformed into hope.

Implications and Actions

There are plenty of things in this world that contribute to hopelessness. Sickness, terrorism, and the sinfulness of our world may make us feel hopeless. When we contemplate our mortality, we may be tempted to think there is no real meaning in life. When Jesus died on the cross, his followers knew the feeling of hopelessness all too well.

But God has raised Jesus from the dead! There is hope because Jesus is alive. Nothing is hopeless for those who follow Jesus. Because God raised Jesus from the dead, there is hope for dead marriages and broken lives. The Bible tells us that, in the end, even the dead in Christ will rise!

The death and resurrection of Jesus Christ give meaning and purpose to our lives. We have salvation from sin because of his death and the hope of eternal life because of his res-urrection. We live for Christ because only in him do we find true hope.

Burial Practices in the Time of Jesus

It was common burial practice to bury a body within hours of death. Spices and fragrances were often used to mask any unpleasant odors. Caretakers wrapped a body in cloth and tied a headscarf under the chin to keep the person's mouth closed.

The body was then placed in a cave for a period until the flesh decayed, leaving only the bones. Then, family members would retrieve the bones and put them in an ossuary, a small stone box. Many ancient ossuaries exist.

Jesus was placed in the tomb for his body to decay. That did not happen! Even before the women could finish putting spices on his body, Jesus rose from the dead.

Case Study

You have been asked to say a few words at the graveside of a friend who has died. The family needs hope. In light of the death and resurrection of Christ, what could you say?

Questions

1. The written notice nailed to Jesus' cross stated the charge against him: "The King of the Jews." What do you think that sign meant to Pilate? the soldiers at the cross? the women at the cross? What do those words mean to you?

2. Why do you think Jesus quoted Psalm 22:1, "My God, my God, why have you forsaken me?" Do you think Jesus thought God had forsaken him?

3. Where do you find hope when you face terrible things in this world (disease, death, terrorism, or financial stress, and so forth)? Does life sometimes seem hopeless? Does the resurrection of Jesus give you hope?

4. How has your faith in the death and resurrection of Christ changed the way you live?

Notes

1. Josephus, *War*, vii 6.4.4.203f.
2. Cicero, *Pro Rabirio* v.16.

Christmas Lesson
God is With Us!

MAIN IDEA

Jesus' birth fulfilled messianic prophecy as he came to be Immanuel, God with us.

QUESTION TO EXPLORE

How should we respond to the fact that Jesus has come to be "God with us?"

STUDY AIM

To respond to Jesus' presence with faith and obedience

QUICK READ

Mary's unexpected pregnancy was not what Joseph had in mind for the beginning of his family life. But through the fulfillment of prophecy and the message of an angel, Joseph discovered the meaning of Christmas: God is with us.

Introduction

For good or ill, Christmas involves family. Most likely you will not be riding over the river and through the woods to grandmother's house in a one-horse open sleigh, but odds are you are going to spend some time with family this Christmas.

Celebrating Christmas with people we love is usually a wonderful thing, a time to enjoy a reunion. Sometimes, however, Christmas with family is stressful. Perhaps you have relatives who do not share your values. Maybe their manners or lifestyle conflict with yours. Like all families, there were good things and bad things about the family into which Jesus was born. For Joseph, family life was stressful, at least at first. But eventually, he got the message of Christmas: God is with us!

Matthew 1:1, 1:17–25

1 A record of the genealogy of Jesus Christ the son of David, the son of Abraham:

• • • • • • • • • • • • • • • • • • •

17 Thus there were fourteen generations in all from Abraham to David, fourteen from David to the exile to Babylon, and fourteen from the exile to the Christ. **18** This is how the birth of Jesus Christ came about: His mother Mary was pledged to be married to Joseph, but before they came together, she was found to be with child through the Holy Spirit. **19** Because Joseph her husband was a righteous man and did not want to expose her to public disgrace, he had in mind to divorce her quietly.

20 But after he had considered this, an angel of the Lord appeared to him in a dream and said, "Joseph son of David, do not be afraid to take Mary home as your wife, because what is conceived in her is from the Holy Spirit. **21** She will give birth to a son, and you are to give him the name Jesus, because he will save his people from their sins."

22 All this took place to fulfill what the Lord had said through the prophet: **23** "The virgin will be with child and will give birth to a son, and they will call him Immanuel" —which means, "God with us."

24 When Joseph woke up, he did what the angel of the Lord had commanded him and took Mary home as his wife. **25** But he had no union with her until she gave birth to a son. And he gave him the name Jesus.

Family Tree (1:1–17)

The Book of Matthew introduces the Christmas story by climbing around in Jesus' family tree. It begins by announcing, "A record of the genealogy of Jesus Christ, the son of David, the son of Abraham." The next fifteen verses tell us more than we ever wanted to know about the relatives of Jesus. It is a strange way to start a story; the action of verse eighteen seems more like a starting point. But genealogies were important to the Jewish people. They reminded them of God's work throughout history to bring about his plan.

This genealogy reminded people of the prophecies about the Messiah coming from the line of David. It reminded them of the covenants God had made with Abraham and how the Messiah was to complete those promises. There is an interesting observation that there were three sets of fourteen generations between Abraham and Jesus, a notation that has had scholars scratching their heads for centuries, but no doubt has theological meaning.

You do need to be careful when you start climbing around in this family tree. There are branches with cracks. You may have some less than savory characters in your family tree as well. Jesus certainly had a few.

There was Rahab, the harlot. She lived in Jericho when Joshua's army attacked. God spared her life because she helped the Hebrew spies. It is surprising enough that Matthew included several women in Jesus' genealogy, but you would think he would leave out the detail that one of Jesus' ancestors was a harlot. But there she is.

David appears in the tree. David was a great king in Israel, and prophets had foretold the Messiah would be from the line of David. But there is an odd addendum to David's name that reminds us David was not always a good guy. David was the father of Solomon "whose mother was Uriah's wife." That would be Bathsheba. David not only committed adultery with her, but had her husband murdered so he could have her. You would think that story would have been pruned out of the family lore of the Messiah.

Manasseh is also mentioned. Manasseh was one of the most wicked and ruthless kings in the history of Israel. And there are other unsavory characters in this family tree. Yet through it all, God was at work. He was carrying out his plan to be with us, even through this less than ideal family tree.

Maybe you are dreading spending time with some of your family members this Christmas. Remember, no matter how unpleasant they are, God is still at work; God is still with us.

Family Crisis (1:18–19)

Jesus' family tree ends with Joseph, his earthly father. Matthew made it clear, though, that Joseph was not Jesus' natural father because Mary was pregnant "before they came together." Mary and Joseph were pledged to be married, but they were not married. The custom of betrothal was more than a modern engagement. In our culture, an engagement can be canceled without repercussions, but a betrothal was a binding contract between families that could only be canceled by a formal divorce. Sexual intimacy was not part of the betrothal but was reserved for the actual marriage, which came later.

Joseph was a righteous man. He knew what God expected of him and others. It must have been an unpleasant surprise to discover Mary's condition. How would he explain this to his mother? Or to her father? It was not his fault. He had obeyed the rules. He had been faithful both to God and Mary. But his lifetime of faithfulness ended in disappointment.

Maybe you have had that kind of experience. You were a good parent who taught Christian values. You took your children to church every week. But they grew up to be scoundrels! Or, maybe you have done everything right in your marriage, but your spouse has rewarded you with unfaithfulness. Or, maybe you have been a faithful servant of the Lord. You are moral. You have gone on mission trips. You have tithed. But a doctor has given you a devastating diagnosis. What do you do when a lifetime of faithfulness ends with disappointment?

For Joseph the answer was obvious. Even in disappointment, he was determined to remain faithful. He had lived a righteous life, and he chose to continue to do so. He trusted that his obedience, even in the face of this crisis, would pay off in the end.

Joseph assumed Mary had committed adultery. Jewish law stated that an adulterous woman could be stoned to death. Fortunately, there was a provision in the law that said the offended husband could divorce her and send her to live in another town, where no one would know of her transgression. Joseph was a man who obeyed the law, but he also had a heart of compassion and would act in the most merciful way possible. He chose to remain faithful to how he perceived God's law.

The Family of God (1:20–25)

One night, while Joseph was sleeping, an angel of God appeared to him in a dream. Dreams have a long history in the Bible as a way of God revealing himself to people. Obviously, we would not want to interpret every dream as God revealing his plan. But before the revelation of God in Christ, God occasionally used dreams to communicate new things. We might recall people like Joseph in the Book of Genesis, or Daniel.

As a reminder of his family tree, the angel called Joseph "Son of David." This reminder would help Joseph make more sense of the message the angel was about to deliver. Prophets had foretold that the Messiah would come from the line of David. Nevertheless, the message from the angel was surprising.

"Do not be afraid to take Mary home as your wife." Joseph had not considered that alternative. It was a possibility that did not exist in the rulebook. In fact, it was against the rules. Considering this alternative must have made Joseph fearful. What would the neighbors think if he took Mary home to be his wife? Would it not be an implicit admission of guilt? Everyone would think he had given up on faithfulness, that he was no longer a righteous man.

The message from the angel was that all of this was a result of God at work in the world. The child Mary carried was the work of the Holy Spirit, and Joseph was to name the child "Jesus." The name "Jesus" is the Greek form of the name "Joshua," which means, "The Lord saves." It would prove to be an appropriate name for the Savior of the world.

The mystery of the virgin birth is more than we can fathom. In our scientific age, this miracle seems inconceivable. It was inconceivable to Joseph as well. Matthew interpreted the virgin birth as a fulfillment of prophecy when he quoted Isaiah 7:14. Although Isaiah was referring to the birth of another child in his day, the Spirit revealed to Matthew that the true fulfillment of prophecy is in Christ.

The child would have the nickname, "Immanuel," which is also a fulfillment of Isaiah's prophecy. "Immanuel" means, "God with us." It is the message of Christmas. God is with us!

It is hard to comprehend that God is with us. God, who created the heavens and the earth, who spoke a word and light came into being, who breathed his breath into lungs of clay and gave life; that God is with us! He did not simply create the world and set it spinning only to leave us alone, nor did God set us out in space and then wait for earth to wind down. God became flesh and lived among us.

Joseph responded by believing this preposterous story. He took Mary home to be his wife, and he named her child "Jesus," just as the angel had commanded. Imagine how hard it must have been to believe. It was hard to have lived a life of righteousness only to be disappointed by the results. Nevertheless, Joseph believed. He chose to live by faith rather than law. He chose to live in relationship with God rather than regulation. He went from trusting rules to trusting God.

Joseph had descended from an imperfect family, and the family he was about to have was not at all what he had imagined. But because he was willing to live by faith, he experienced God with us.

Implications and Actions

Today is Christmas. Your Christmas may not be perfect this year. It will be marred by family members who are not there and for some, it may be marred by family members who are there. In the midst of imperfection, God is with us. When the children are whining they did not get the presents they wanted, God is with us. When the crass uncle is telling inappropriate jokes that make your skin crawl, God is with us. When an empty chair is staring at you because of the death of a loved one, God is with us. It is, after all, what Christmas is all about. It is the preposterous story Joseph heard from an angel. Immanuel: God is with us.

The History of Betrothal

Mary and Joseph were betrothed but not yet married. A betrothal was a legal and binding contract, often arranged by the parents of their children, and consummated later after the wedding. Betrothal was as binding as marriage and could be dissolved only by legal divorce.

Betrothed couples did not engage in sexual activity until after the wedding. The Bible indicates that Mary and Joseph did not live together until after they were officially married, nor did they engage in sexual activity until after the birth of Jesus.

Joseph's decision to quietly divorce Mary was a merciful alternative to the possibility of stoning her for her suspected adultery. At first, Joseph must have thought divorce was the only merciful choice. God showed him another way.

The Apostle Paul used the metaphor of betrothal in 2 Corinthians 11:2 when he sought to explain the church as a virgin bride presented to Christ.

Case Study

Your friend has told you that God told her she was supposed to marry a man who is not a Christ-follower and has a scandalous reputation. How can you help her recognize a message from God as opposed to listening to her desires?

Questions

1. How have your ancestors affected the person you are today? How have they influenced your faith either for good or bad? How can you positively influence the lives your descendants?

2. How does Joseph's response to the angel's message provide an example for our response to God? Does this mean any dream or intuition should be viewed as a message from God even if it conflicts with our understanding of Scripture?

3. Discuss how the message of Christmas—God is with us—can help you in times of disappointment and fear.

4. If God is with us, how can we explain the terrible things that happen in this world? If God is with us, why do bad things happen?

Our Next New Study
(Available for use beginning March 2017)

POWER & PURPOSE:
God Unveils the Universe
A STUDY OF GENESIS 1–11

HOW TO ORDER
More Bible Study Materials

It's easy! Just fill in the following information. For additional Bible study materials available both in print and digital versions, see www.baptistwaypress.org, or get a catalog by calling 1-866-249-1799 or e-mailing baptistway@texasbaptists.org.

━━━ PLEASE NOTE ━━━

In addition to these Bible studies, which are available in both print and digital formats, we have several studies available in a digital-only format. See www.baptistwaypress.org for a complete listing of these studies.

Title of item	Price	Quantity	Cost
This Issue			
On Your Mark: The Gospel in Motion (Mark)—Study Guide (BWP001227)	$4.25	_____	_____
On Your Mark: The Gospel in Motion (Mark)—Large Print Study Guide (BWP001228)	$4.50	_____	_____
On Your Mark: The Gospel in Motion (Mark)—Teaching Guide (BWP001229)	$4.95	_____	_____
Additional Issues Available			
Faith > Fear—Study Guide (BWP001217)	$4.25	_____	_____
Faith > Fear—Large Print Study Guide (BWP001218)	$4.50	_____	_____
Faith > Fear—Teaching Guide (BWP001219)	$4.95	_____	_____
Created for Relationships—Study Guide (BWP001197)	$3.95	_____	_____
Created for Relationships—Large Print Study Guide (BWP001198)	$4.25	_____	_____
Created for Relationships—Teaching Guide (BWP001199)	$4.95	_____	_____
14 Habits of Highly Effective Disciples—Study Guide (BWP001177)	$3.95	_____	_____
14 Habits of Highly Effective Disciples—Large Print Study Guide (BWP001178)	$4.25	_____	_____
14 Habits of Highly Effective Disciples—Teaching Guide (BWP001179)	$4.95	_____	_____
Guidance for the Seasons of Life—Study Guide (BWP001157)	$3.95	_____	_____
Guidance for the Seasons of Life—Large Print Study Guide (BWP001158)	$4.25	_____	_____
Guidance for the Seasons of Life—Teaching Guide (BWP001159)	$4.95	_____	_____
Old Testament			
Exodus: Liberated for Life in Covenant with God—Study Guide (BWP001192)	$3.95	_____	_____
Exodus: Liberated for Life in Covenant with God—Large Print Study Guide (BWP001193)	$4.25	_____	_____
Exodus: Liberated for Life in Covenant with God—Teaching Guide (BWP001194)	$4.95	_____	_____
Choices and Consequences (Joshua/Judges)—Study Guide (BWP001212)	$4.25	_____	_____
Choices and Consequences (Joshua/Judges)—Large Print Study Guide (BWP001213)	$4.50	_____	_____
Choices and Consequences (Joshua/Judges)—Teaching Guide (BWP001214)	$4.95	_____	_____
Psalms: Songs from the Heart of Faith—Study Guide (BWP001152)	$3.95	_____	_____
Psalms: Songs from the Heart of Faith—Large Print Study Guide (BWP001153)	$4.25	_____	_____
Psalms: Songs from the Heart of Faith—Teaching Guide (BWP001154)	$4.95	_____	_____
Jeremiah and Ezekiel: Prophets of Judgment and Hope—Study Guide (BWP001172)	$3.95	_____	_____
Jeremiah and Ezekiel: Prophets of Judgment and Hope—Large Print Study Guide (BWP001173)	$4.25	_____	_____
Jeremiah and Ezekiel: Prophets of Judgment and Hope—Teaching Guide (BWP001174)	$4.95	_____	_____
New Testament			
Jesus: King or Concierge? (Matthew)—Study Guide (BWP001207)	$4.25	_____	_____
Jesus: King or Concierge? (Matthew)—Large Print Study Guide (BWP001208)	$4.50	_____	_____
Jesus: King or Concierge? (Matthew)—Teaching Guide (BWP001209)	$4.95	_____	_____
The Gospel of Luke: Jesus' Personal Touch—Study Guide (BWP001167)	$3.95	_____	_____
The Gospel of Luke: Jesus' Personal Touch—Large Print Study Guide (BWP001168)	$4.25	_____	_____
The Gospel of Luke: Jesus' Personal Touch—Teaching Guide (BWP001169)	$4.95	_____	_____
The Gospel of John: Believe in Jesus and Live!—Study Guide (BWP001187)	$3.95	_____	_____
The Gospel of John: Believe in Jesus and Live!—Large Print Study Guide (BWP001188)	$4.25	_____	_____
The Gospel of John: Believe in Jesus and Live!—Teaching Guide (BWP001189)	$4.95	_____	_____

Romans: A Gospel-Centered Worldview—Study Guide (BWP001202)	$4.25	_____ _____
Romans: A Gospel-Centered Worldview—Large Print Study Guide (BWP001203)	$4.50	_____ _____
Romans: A Gospel-Centered Worldview—Teaching Guide (BWP001204)	$4.95	_____ _____
Letters to the Ephesians and Timothy—Study Guide (BWP001182)	$3.95	_____ _____
Letters to the Ephesians and Timothy—Large Print Study Guide (BWP001183)	$4.25	_____ _____
Letters to the Ephesians and Timothy—Teaching Guide (BWP001184)	$4.95	_____ _____
Hebrews and the Letters of Peter—Study Guide (BWP001162)	$3.95	_____ _____
Hebrews and the Letters of Peter—Large Print Study Guide (BWP001163)	$4.25	_____ _____
Hebrews and the Letters of Peter—Teaching Guide (BWP001164)	$4.95	_____ _____
Terror and Triumph (Revelation)—Study Guide (BWP001222)	$4.25	_____ _____
Terror and Triumph (Revelation)—Large Print Study Guide (BWP001223)	$4.50	_____ _____
Terror and Triumph (Revelation)—Teaching Guide (BWP001224)	$4.95	_____ _____

Coming for use beginning March 2017

Power & Purpose: God Unveils the Universe (Genesis 1-11)—Study Guide (BWP001232)	$4.25	_____ _____
Power & Purpose: God Unveils the Universe (Genesis 1-11)—Large Print Study Guide (BWP001233)	$4.50	_____ _____
Power & Purpose: God Unveils the Universe (Genesis 1-11)—Teaching Guide (BWP001234)	$4.95	_____ _____

Standard (UPS/Mail) Shipping Charges*			
Order Value	Shipping charge**	Order Value	Shipping charge**
$.01–$9.99	$6.50	$160.00–$199.99	$24.00
$10.00–$19.99	$8.50	$200.00–$249.99	$28.00
$20.00–$39.99	$9.50	$250.00–$299.99	$30.00
$40.00–$59.99	$10.50	$300.00–$349.99	$34.00
$60.00–$79.99	$11.50	$350.00–$399.99	$42.00
$80.00–$99.99	$12.50	$400.00–$499.99	$50.00
$100.00–$129.99	$15.00	$500.00–$599.99	$60.00
$130.00–$159.99	$20.00	$600.00–$799.99	$72.00**

Cost of items (Order value) _____

Shipping charges (see chart*) _____

TOTAL _____

*Please call 1-866-249-1799 if the exact amount is needed prior to ordering.

**For order values $800.00 and above, please call 1-866-249-1799 or check www.baptistwaypress.org

Please allow two weeks for standard delivery.
For express shipping service: Call 1-866-249-1799 for information on additional charges.

YOUR NAME   PHONE

YOUR CHURCH   DATE ORDERED

SHIPPING ADDRESS

CITY   STATE   ZIP CODE

E-MAIL

MAIL this form with your check for the total amount to:
BAPTISTWAY PRESS, Baptist General Convention of Texas,
7557 Rambler Road, Suite 1200, Dallas, TX 75231–2388
(Make checks to "BaptistWay Press")

OR, **CALL** your order toll-free: 1-866-249-1799
(M-Fri 8:30 a.m.-5:00 p.m. central time).

OR, **E-MAIL** your order to: baptistway@texasbaptists.org.

OR, **ORDER ONLINE** at www.baptistwaypress.org.

We look forward to receiving your order! Thank you!